Loving My Children

Embracing Biblical Motherhood

KATIE FARIS

To my first love, the Lord Jesus Christ;
my greatest earthly love, Scott;
and our little loves:
Elijah, John Luke, Silas and Selah

Loving My Children

Published by Faris Press
P.O. Box 90
Riverton, New Jersey 08077
Visit www.farispress.com

Edited by Scott Faris
Cover design by Katie Faris

Faris, Katie.
Loving My Children: Embracing Biblical Motherhood
ISBN-13: 978-0-6159-7552-8
ISBN-10: 0-615-97552-6

FARIS PRESS

CONTENTS

THANKS

I'm grateful for my mom, my mother-in-love, and the many Titus 2 ladies who have humbly listened to, counseled, encouraged and prayed for me over the years. Thank you for loving God, loving his Word and adorning the Gospel by the way you love your families. You've walked before me and walked with me, and I wouldn't be who I am without you.

Special thanks to the ladies of Sovereign Grace Church in Marlton, New Jersey, who embrace biblical motherhood so beautifully. It is a joy to love Jesus and love our children together.

Finally, in loving memory of Kathy Hinton, a Titus 2 friend who went to be with Jesus on July 30, 2011.

I thank my God in all my remembrance of you.
Philippians 1:3

FOREWORD

I love my wife. Katie is kind, godly, beautiful and gentle. She's also a capable thinker and writer, and she's much better at relating her weaknesses to others than I am. As you read, you'll benefit from her transparency. She wrote this book because she wanted to understand what it means to love our children biblically.

Doing so meant looking to Scripture and the example of others. By God's kindness and mercy, we've benefited from the gift of being around Christian parents and mentors older and more experienced in applying God's Word to life than we are, as well as loving friends who have walked alongside us. These dear people have been generous with their time and wisdom. They've also been honest about their failures, and it's the treasure of their experience and instruction that Katie freely shares with you.

Parenting isn't easy, and challenges abound. John Bunyan, author of *The Pilgrim's Progress,* penned another story of heavenward struggle, *The Holy War*. In its introduction, Bunyan speaks of people who "can with tears and joy the story tell." His words paint an accurate picture of the nature of our spiritual journey.

Since this book was written, Katie and I have encountered our share of unexpected trials. Most notably, we discovered that some of our children have serious medical conditions. Within months, our calendar was filled with phone calls and visits to doctors, specialists and researchers. Learning to apply God's Word to this new dimension of parenting was beyond what we had planned or imagined.

But in the midst of these challenges, God has been very, very good to us. As this book has developed, we've found that the biblical truths it champions have been put to the test in real, profound ways. The outcome? We can testify that God's Word is indeed sufficient, more than equal to the task of helping weak, needy sinners such as us raise our children.

We trust that beyond any human means of grace, God's Word and the Holy Spirit will equip you to face the mounting challenges of parenting in modern times. The counsel of God's Word stands strong and immovable, and the Lord never, ever fails those he loves.

Scott Faris
Riverton, New Jersey
July 2015

CHAPTER ONE

Love at First Sight?

My first moments with my newborn babies were precious. I never want to forget those first kisses or the sweetness of sheltering their swaddled bodies close to my heart and soothing their new-to-this-world cries with songs of comfort. What a humbling, awesome thing it was to pull those little ones close and realize, "This is *my* baby–not a doll, not a friend's baby, but *my* baby."

As long as I can remember, I've wanted to be a mother. When my first child was born, I entered into my new role with joyful enthusiasm. Not only did the Lord fill my heart with love for my son, Elijah, but he filled my heart with increased admiration and love for my husband as I watched his heart open to our newborn.

My love was real, and it was a gift. As the Lord has added more children to our family, I'm amazed how this love has multiplied and expanded, growing my heart and affections for each of our children. By God's grace, I am a blessed woman, and I love my children.

Perhaps you, too, have always wanted to be a mother. Or maybe not. No matter how you entered motherhood, if you've been a mom for any length of time you'll probably agree that it's not for the faint of heart! There are days when the ocean of motherhood is calm, and I enjoy the reflection of the sun shining on my face as I swim through its waters. Then there are days when I feel like it's sucking me into the deep, and I'm thrashing to stay afloat.

But I don't think that I've ever just sat on the beach in a lounge chair with a cool drink watching the waves roll to shore. Being a mom is not a vacation or a spectator sport. As moms, we're in the water with our kids. Motherhood requires our full participation.

Motherhood is also extremely sanctifying. Despite the very real roots of love established in those early days, it's taken more than love at first sight to endure the everyday trials and temptations of motherhood. What do I do when my toddler decides to color with permanent markers on the living room couch, or another child throws a tantrum in the children's section of the library? What about times I find syrup (or glue or baby powder) decorating my carpet? I need love that is more than a feeling. I need the kind of love that Paul described when he wrote the biblical command that instructs older women to "train the young women to love their husbands and children" (Titus 2:4). This kind of love has to be taught, and is therefore something Scripture says we are to learn.

MOTHERHOOD 101

For my husband, Scott, and me, our first year of marriage was full of change. Not only were we newlyweds, but I very soon became pregnant and gave birth to our first child, Elijah. Then, Scott left a good job to prepare for full-time pastoral ministry. One month after celebrating our first anniversary, we packed up our apartment, took our three-month-old and moved from New Jersey to Maryland to share a home with a family we had never met so that Scott could attend a nearby Pastors College.

I learned so much in that first year of motherhood as I cared for my baby in the home of a family that would become very dear to us—Jim and Marianne and their three school-age children. Not only did I have a loving mother and mother-in-law who were only a phone call away, but I had a godly, experienced woman living in the same house with me, someone whom I could ask questions of and seek counsel from. I would ask her things like, "What do I do when Elijah doesn't want to eat his baby food?" "Do you think he might be teething?" "When do I call the doctor if I think my baby is sick?" Help was right at hand with

Marianne. With her, I also had a front-row seat to see real motherly love in action as she cared for her children.

When Titus 2:4 talks about loving our children, the adjectival form of the Greek word *phileo* is used. I'm not a Greek scholar, and I'm not planning to use any other Greek words in this book. However, I needed to make sure that I was headed in the right direction in understanding this command to "love" in Scripture as it relates to children, so I studied this word a bit.

Here's what I found out: *phileo* functions similarly to the English word for "love," and, like that word in our own language, it can express a lot of different things depending on the context in which it is used. So, when we read in the Bible that older women are to teach younger women how to "love" their children (and husbands), it means that they're really teaching them how to train and discipline their children, to understand their children, to treat their children with affection and kindness, to welcome and befriend their children, to be fond of them, and even to kiss them. Motherly love encompasses a whole range of actions and motives. That's what it means to love our offspring in a Titus 2-kind-of-way.

Living in Marianne's home, I saw her do all of these things. She scheduled special times with her daughter on the calendar, hugged and encouraged her boys, admonished her children gently and privately, laughed with them, came alongside them in doing chores and played games with them. At that time, she homeschooled them, giving the best part of her day and energies to teaching them. I observed a mom who genuinely enjoyed being with her children.

But Marianne's love for her children didn't simply spring from natural affection. Each morning, I also watched her wake up before the rest of her family, slip downstairs to make a cup of tea and then close the door to the school room so that she could read her Bible and pray. Marianne found the strength to love her children from knowing that she was loved by God.

In Isaiah 40:11, the prophet Isaiah describes the Lord as a shepherd who "gently [leads] those that are with young." Marianne's life and friendship was just one of the ways that the Lord gently led me as a new mom. There have been so many women whose examples have influenced and shaped my thinking about motherhood that I can't give all the credit where it is due. All I can say is this: everything I'm writing about here comes from what I've heard, read or seen modeled by someone else.

ONE CRAZY, NEEDY LADY

I don't think I know all there is to know about loving my children, and I certainly don't believe that I'm the best person to teach about it. In fact, if I could boil down my prayers as a mom of young children to one word, that word would be "Help!"

I distinctly remember bowing my head next to my husband at the side of our bed in the middle of the night during those first weeks of parenting. Elijah was crying hard, without stopping, and after feeding and changing and holding him, we didn't know what else to do but pray for him. And God answered those prayers and helped our son. As the years have gone by, the Lord continues to humble us by revealing our dependence on him for wisdom in parenting, especially in desperate times.

I began writing this book when I was seven months pregnant with our third child. Yes, a bit crazy, I know. But it was God's perfect timing for my heart. Even though I'd only been a mom for four years, it had been long enough for me to begin to understand that biblical love wasn't coming naturally to me.

In the months before I started writing, I found myself caught in a web of sinfully comparing my two young boys to other children and setting undue expectations on them, especially given their capacities and levels of maturity. I would often give in to anger, self-pity and fear when they did not conform to my desires and demands. The Lord mercifully convicted my heart as he helped me to understand the biblical definition of love.

Colossians 3 teaches us to "put off" sin and "put on" attributes that befit God's children. Not only did he graciously open my eyes to see the sins that had so easily entangled me, and which I needed to "put off," but he also began showing me what I was to "put on" in place of those sin patterns.

The Lord gave me a desire to learn what it means to love my children biblically, and the best way I could think to do this was to study Scripture and consider the examples of wiser, more experienced women. A lot has changed in our family since this book was first written, and it hasn't always been easy. Yet the Lord is faithful, and he continues to work for good in fulfilling his purposes and plans in our lives.

Finally, although I wrote this book primarily for myself and for moms with young children, I certainly want to include all moms, including moms-to-be and mothers of older children. If you are waiting to be a mother someday and are reading this book, that's wonderful! Praise God for giving you a heart to love children now. May he use the words of this book to help you love your nieces and nephews, neighborhood children and children in your church; help you come alongside your friends with small children; and prepare your heart for children he may give you in the future.

If your children are older, I commend you, too. Thank you for being humble and reading a book by someone who isn't as far along in her journey and for your example of wanting to love your children better. Let's face it, we all need to be encouraged to love our children better, no matter what our season of motherhood is! And, if this is you, perhaps there is a less experienced mother in your life that the Lord wants you to encourage.

Whoever you are and whatever your season of life, if you, like me, find that the longer you're a mom, the more you need Jesus, my hope and prayer is that you'll find something helpful and be encouraged as you read.

CHAPTER TWO

The Best Way to Love My Children

One of the things that my husband and I like to do when we celebrate our wedding anniversary is watch the video of our wedding day. It's always fun to see the big grin on Scott's face as he jogs to the front of the church wearing his T-shirt and shorts with his tuxedo slung over his shoulder. There's also a poignant picture where I'm showing my grandmother the pearl that I'm wearing around my neck, her gift to me from many years earlier. Even though Alzheimer's had taken its toll on her body and mind, in that moment I was convinced that she knew it was a special day for me.

One year, we made a family event out of watching the wedding. It certainly wasn't a Hollywood hit, because Elijah fell asleep halfway through! As we fast-forwarded parts of the ceremony and the reception, we relived one of our favorite elements of that day: a time when we honored our parents. Many of the guests at our wedding knew our families well, and it was a privilege to take time to publicly describe how our parents led us by word and example as we grew up.

Scott has said that in his home, it was as if the air you breathed had the Gospel in it. Both of his parents, Dave and Bev, love the Lord, and Scott grew up as the heir of a rich Christian heritage. With his father as a pastor, much of his family life was also interwoven with the life of the church. By the time we were married, his dad had served as a pastor for more than 40 years.

Scott's mom played a critical role in his conversion. He remembers being sick and staying home from a Sunday evening church service with her. As he was lying on the floor staring up at the ceiling, he started thinking about heaven and hell and death. Questions flowed, and Bev discerned the significance of the moment. She set aside the dishes she was washing in the kitchen, talked with her son, and led him to Jesus.

My parents are also Christians, and our church was a huge part of our lives. When I was close to five years old, I heard a pastor preach about my need for forgiveness for my sins and the salvation that was available to me through Jesus Christ's death on the cross. I went home, knelt down beside the living room couch and prayed, asking Jesus to come into my heart. And then I prayed again. I confessed to a friend later that I prayed that "sinner's prayer" a dozen or more times, just to make sure it really stuck!

Although our respective understandings of sin and grace and our need for Christ were incomplete and very immature at those young ages, God was at work. By his grace, he placed us in homes that nurtured and encouraged our faith to grow.

Scott and I grew up in homes where it was normal to talk about God, where prayer was a daily practice and our parents did their best to point us to the Lord. As a young girl, if I crept downstairs early in the morning, I knew I'd find my father reading his Bible and praying for our family. Growing up with Christian parents was a gift that neither Scott nor I ever want to take for granted. They shaped homes where we were exposed to the Gospel and saw it lived out practically every day. The gift of a godly (not perfect) context doesn't save anyone or give any advantage in terms of standing with God–God's grace alone determines that. But the gift of it remains, all for a purpose.

THE GOSPEL IS PRIMARY

Shouldn't I save the best part for last? Leave my readers on the edge of their seats? The truth is, if you take away one thing from reading this book, I want it to be this: The best way that we can love our children is by passing on the Gospel to them. That's it. I hope you don't stop reading here, but if you do, you've gotten the most important thing you need to know.

Loving my children isn't about whether I breastfeed or bottle-feed. It's not about whether or not I let my daughter eat refined sugar before she's two, or she never gets sugar at all. It's not even about whether I choose to homeschool, enroll my child in a public school or send him or her to a private school. These decisions and the convictions behind them are important, but they're not the Gospel. They don't carry an ultimate weight exclusive to its claims.

So, what is the Gospel? You can fail every other test in life, but this is the one question demanding a crystal-clear answer. Paul states it plainly in 1 Corinthians 15:3: "Christ died for our sins." These five words are very simple, like learning the five vowels in English. You can count one word on each finger of one hand. At bedtime, we've made a practice of saying this simple Gospel summary together with our children because we want it to be emblazoned on their minds.

These five, simple words embody the most profound, life-changing and powerful truth in the world, a truth that's simple enough for a child to understand and one that also confounds the greatest scholars. Why would Jesus Christ, the perfect Son of God, take on human flesh and live a blameless, sinless life in order to become my substitute, to pay for my sins by bearing them as he died on the cross? I don't have a comprehensive answer to that question, and no one else seems to, either. It is a deep, abiding mystery.

But the good news of this Gospel is clear, and in the glory of Christ's death on our behalf is where we learn the nature of true love. First John 3:16 says, "By this we know love, that he laid down his life for us, and we ought to lay down our lives for the brothers." Any biblical discussion about loving our children needs to begin with the demonstrated love that Jesus showed us when he died. Not only does that love enable me to truly love my children—because I've been loved and forgiven by the one who laid down his life for me—but it motivates, informs and guides how I am to lay down my life for my children. It teaches me the sacrificial quality of the love I'm called to, a love that doesn't get its power from within myself. The power to love must come—like our salvation—from the Lord, from his Spirit living in us.

Then how do we love our children this way? I want to suggest three ways. First, we can teach our children the Gospel itself, helping them taste and see the great truth and reality of it. Next, we can love the Gospel ourselves, from grateful, humble hearts. Finally, we can pray for them.

TEACH THE GOSPEL

First, we teach them. We must make sure that by the time our children grow up, they leave our homes with a clear understanding of the Gospel's content and its claims. From Genesis to Revelation, the story of the Bible is the story of God at work saving a people for himself. Everything written in God's Word either anticipates the coming of Jesus, tells the story of his time on earth, records the impact of his resurrection or points to his future return. Woven throughout the Old Testament are stories of people whose lives serve as "types" of the coming Messiah, pointing to his coming. In the New Testament, we read about men and women who were transformed through their encounters with Jesus Christ.

If we're going to teach the Gospel to our children, then we need to be students of the entire Bible. They do not need just to know about God, but must learn to know God and his son, Jesus, our Savior who came to save sinners and who will come again to judge and rule forever. Does how we talk about Jesus reveal to our children who he really is?

I once read a short booklet that talked about how we often sacrifice the "important" things in our lives for urgent things. In the midst of the many urgent tasks of mothering young children (like potty training and preparing food), it's easy to neglect the study of God's Word. But it's the Bible that informs our lives and tells us what we're supposed to talk to our children about. As moms, we need to make sure that we're prioritizing a regular time of reading it and having time to consider and apply it. This also means taking the time to think carefully about and heed what God says to us in the preaching of his Word.

As a mom, I know how hard this can be! My time reading the Bible looks much different as a mom with young children than it did when I was a single woman. Sunday mornings at church can feel like a distracted marathon of care. This is where I love the example of Jesus in Matthew 14. If you read through that chapter, you see that Jesus keeps trying to get away from the crowds to spend time with God, but the people keep finding him and he has compassion on them when they do. Eventually he finds some time alone, but it isn't until the evening.

I have a lot of days like that. After being up in the middle of the night with my children, I roll out of bed at the same time they do. We jump into the day's activities and I'm grabbing for moments alone with Jesus—a quiet minute to pray in the bathroom, five minutes of Bible reading while the kids play, and maybe singing along with some worship music while I make lunch. I've had a lot of "quiet times" while feeding my children. I think the important questions are ones concerning the heart: Do I want to be with the Lord? Am I asking him for time? Am I seizing the moments he gives me? Then, when our children need our attention, we can feel complete freedom to show them compassion and take care of them. We also have a better perspective when we do.

How else do we teach the Gospel? God's Word isn't meant to be merely an intellectual exercise. We need to talk about God's Word with our children in the midst of day-to-day living. In the Old Testament, Moses gives us a picture of how all-encompassing educating our children really is. He says, "The LORD our God, the LORD is one. You shall love the LORD your God with all your heart and with all your soul and with all your might. And these words that I command you today shall be on your heart. You shall teach them diligently to your children, and shall talk of them when you sit in your house, and when you walk by the way, and when you lie down, and when you rise" (Deut. 6:4-5, 7). Do you see it? Anywhere and everywhere (not just in church or on Sundays), all the time, we're to be talking about God with our children. In our homes, in our cars and on the playground, we're to be talking about who God is. It's so clear, and yet so hard to actually do in our modern world.

Our conversation isn't limited to mere descriptions of God's character, though. We're also supposed to talk about what he's done. God's character leads him to action, and his works require a response from us. Psalm 145 is a crescendo of celebration of God's wondrous works and mighty deeds. It extols his character and glory. In verse four, David writes, "One generation shall commend your works to another, and shall declare your mighty acts." The Gospel is God's greatest work on behalf of mankind, and of all God's works, it is the one most worthy to be commended to our children. If they get nothing else from us, let them get this. If we talk about nothing else, let's talk about the Good News. We don't just want to cram a lot of information into our children's heads; we want the Gospel to be inscribed on their hearts and extolled in their worship of God. But how do we flesh out this Gospel and make it alive in front of them?

LOVE THE GOSPEL MYSELF

I once heard well-known Christian speaker and writer Jerry Bridges preach on the power of example, and he referenced parenting. The gist of what he was teaching that day was this: when it comes to parenting and the Gospel, how you live out the Gospel can be even more important than what you say about the Gospel. Simply put, if you speak Gospel words but don't apply them personally, those words are not going to mean much to your children. In fact, there's a good chance that they'll leave home someday thinking you're a hypocrite and that there really isn't much substance to the Christian faith.

However, if you live out the Gospel in front of them in a transparent and humble way—even if they don't agree with you in a given season or phase—they won't be able to argue with the integrity of your example. "But I'm weak and imperfect," you say. There's good news for that fact: Jesus didn't die for so-called "godly" people, but he died for the ungodly. Romans 5:8 says, "But God shows his love for us in that while we were still sinners, Christ died for us."

Our children know that we're not perfect. If they're familiar with biblical vocabulary, they know that we are all sinners. No matter how much we'd like to hide that fact, we can't. But as sinners saved by God's grace, we have the amazing privilege of displaying the Gospel to our children in weakness and sin and error. When we mess up and fail in our parenting, we have a merciful Savior who is ready to forgive us. Because we've been forgiven much, we can forgive others much. Because we've been loved extravagantly, we can love with abandon, even when our children treat us as enemies, or so it seems sometimes. Do our children get to see us give and receive forgiveness? Do they even know that we fail and need it?

So much in modern life is measured against performance that the economy of God's love and his generosity to sinners who woefully underperform and offend God's holiness can seem shocking, even scandalous. Could he really love us that much? The fact is, he does, and he calls us to do the same for others, beginning with our spouses and children. Charity—in the truest and most biblical sense of that word—really does begin at home.

Not only does the Gospel speak to and meet our greatest needs as parents, but it also motivates the way we love our children. Most of our children may not yet be converted, but we love them "while [they are] still sinners," with the same love with which Christ loved us before we came to a saving knowledge of the Gospel. When my toddler throws a tantrum, I don't want to leave him in his sinful mess. I might need to remove him from the public eye, but I want to hold him, pray over him, speak truth to him, sing over him and whisper in his ear that I'm for him and not against him.

The best books on Christian parenting account for mercy, even when sin is being addressed. And when discipline is in order, I want to do my very best to communicate the same mercy, love, patience and perseverance to my children that my Savior shows me every day.

So, we should ask ourselves some questions. Do I know and believe the Gospel? Do I love the Gospel—the fact that I am a sinner saved from God's wrath because he poured it out on Jesus instead? Do I live like I'm forgiven (and do I forgive others), or do I walk with a heavy burden of guilt on my shoulders (and withhold forgiveness from others)? Do I celebrate my salvation with a joyful spirit? Do my children know that I love Jesus and that if everything else were taken away from me, the Lord would be enough? Am I eager to share the Gospel with others, and do my children see and hear me sharing Good News with others? Do I talk like someone who's been changed by God's power, speaking humbly, kindly, gently, wisely, and gratefully?

God intends for the Gospel to be more than knowledge that we affirmed once upon a time. The glorious truth of forgiveness of sins and hope in Jesus is meant to affect our daily lives. If it does, our children will know. And, if this hope is absent, they will know that as well.

An example I love: when our church accepts new members, our pastor usually reminds those gathered up front that the greatest contribution they can make to the life of the church is their personal godliness. More than serving on any ministry team, the best way they can serve the church is by loving God and growing in their relationship with their Savior, loving Him more and more and growing in faith. In a similar way, I have to say that there are many ways I serve my children; I cook, clean, give baths, teach the alphabet and read to them. Like most mothers, I do a lot for my children, and often wish I could do more. But, more importantly, I can give my children the example of a mother who loves and lives for Jesus, cherishing and demonstrating his Gospel before their watching eyes. There is great value in that kind of example.

PRAY FOR THEM

One of the most humbling discoveries to me as a parent is that even though Scott and I do our best to provide and care for our children, we cannot save their souls. Only God can give them the critical gift of faith in Christ: "For by grace you have been saved through faith. And this is not your own doing; it is the gift of God, not a result of works, so that no one may boast" (Eph. 2:8-9). I cannot do any good work or deed that will achieve for my children the end goal of their salvation. That means that if they are saved and live fruitful lives for Jesus, I won't be able to boast in anything that I said or did along the way to "get them there." All of it will be God's work, and all will be for his glory.

While I was expecting Elijah (my firstborn), I prayed for the little one growing inside my womb. I searched the Bible for verses on children and parenting, and then I wrote them down on index cards. Next, I put them into my own words as prayers. I would flip through these cards on a regular basis, praying for my unborn child. One of the things I prayed over and over again was for his salvation, and a favorite verse was Psalm 102:28, "The children of your servants shall dwell secure; their offspring shall be established before you." I would pray, Lord Jesus, our hope and prayer is that our child will come to know you as his Lord and Savior at a young age. In your mercy, please extend the gift of salvation to him. O Lord, may he live in your presence and be established as one who walks with you by faith.

As a mom with young children, one of the sweetest blessings I've experienced is meeting with a small group of moms in the same season of life to pray together for our children. While our prayers vary between gatherings, almost every time, my friend Julie prays for the salvation of these children. And it's right that she does.

In the same way that we can talk with our children about God all the time and anywhere, we can pray for our children all the time, anywhere—whether they're home or at school, unborn or getting ready to be married. In fact, Paul encouraged the Thessalonians to "pray without ceasing" (1 Thes. 5:17), and this is certainly true for mothers. Inspired by British preacher C.H. Spurgeon, my friend Betsy prays that her children would be "holy, humble and happy." Moms pray for their children for salvation, purity, godly spouses, protection, wisdom, jobs—the list goes on. We may not be able to save our children's souls and be masters of their destinies—earthly or eternal—but we can certainly intercede for them.

CHAPTER THREE

The Best Gift I Can Give My Children

My affection for my husband grew exponentially in our first weeks of parenthood. It caught me totally off-guard! But, when I saw Scott hold Elijah and smile into his face, my heart leaped. It was like falling in love with my husband all over again.

The same passage in the book of Titus that instructs mothers to love their children also addresses how women are to relate to their husbands. Paul instructs older Christian women to "...train the young women to love their husbands and children" (Titus 2:4). Both are important.

Entire books have been written on this topic, and while I don't want to exhaust the subject or get diverted from our theme of loving our children, I do want to focus briefly on how loving one's husband is a crucial way that women can love their children. If the best way to love your children is to pass the Gospel on to them, consider this the *next* best way. John Wooden, a well-known basketball coach famous for his maxims, once said that the best thing a man could ever do for his children would be to love their mother. I'd like to modify that statement and say that the best gift a woman can give to her children is to love their father.

LOVING MY HUSBAND: A STORY

Similar to how I'm exhorted to love my children, God's Word also teaches me to love and respect my husband. When Scott and I were in our courtship, it was a season of learning to love one another, like one another, treat one another with kindness, welcome and befriend one another. There were other critical components to our love and friendship as well, but that's what love would need to look like for a good marriage foundation. Actually being married took this kind of love to a whole new level. But, before I go any further, let me tell you our love story.

Scott and I have been teased excessively due to the fact that we first met when he was eighteen and I was ten—and he was teaching my Sunday school class! He gets ribbed by his friends about "robbing the cradle." If you were to ask our moms, our story is one of God's kindness and grace— and much answered prayer. When Scott's father came to pastor the small church my family attended, we never would have guessed that the Farises' youngest son would one day marry the Thompsons' oldest daughter.

After the Lord directed each of our lives in very different ways over the fifteen years that followed our initial encounter, we re-met in what might seem an unlikely place: China! Scott was teaching in a private school near Hong Kong, and I was teaching at a homeschool co-op for international students in central China. One holiday, he visited some mutual friends of ours in the city where I lived. I greeted him with chocolate chip cookies, and as they say, "the rest is history."

Over the next year, we only saw one another one more time in Asia, and we only exchanged a few emails. So I had no idea how interested Scott was becoming in me until I came back to the United States for a summer visit and found what has become known as the legendary "Long Letter" waiting for me.

With my dad's blessing, Scott poured out his heart in this letter, asking if I would consider a courtship with him. My heart thrilled with this news. Was this God's answer to my prayer for a godly husband? Within a week, Scott arrived for a short visit with me and my family. A few days later, I agreed to a courtship. A month down the road, we made the decision that both of us would remain in the United States rather than return to China so we could get to know one another better in the context of family and friends.

By the end of that summer, Scott finished graduate school and relocated to live close to my family in New Jersey. We found a church together and both started looking for jobs. Although I cared deeply for Scott, and he made so many significant decisions in order to pursue me the way he did, I didn't say "yes" to marriage right away. It took time to get to know one another. While I had always admired him, I had never spent so much time with him. We had both acted independently as singles for several years, and I found myself asking, "Can I be led by this man? Can I follow him, submit to him?"

We didn't fall in love with one another overnight (at least I didn't with him; apparently, he fell for me a lot sooner). Over time, the Lord answered my questions and deepened my affections for Scott. I loved him, and I was ready to marry him. He asked, I said yes, we married, and as we live life together with our growing family, my love for him only increases.

A GOSPEL PORTRAIT

While Scott and I have our own love story, our married love is actually part of something much bigger than the two of us, something deeply and profoundly theological. I can't separate Paul's instruction that young women love their husbands in Titus 2 from Paul's exposition of marriage in Ephesians 5:22-33. As moms, our children hear what we say both to and about our husbands. They see whether or not we're excited when our husbands come home in the evening. They watch when the babysitter comes over so Mommy and Daddy can go out on a date. They search faces and words to see if their parents really love one another. This lived-out kind of love isn't just important because it gives children security and stability (which it certainly does), but it's important because even before children comprehend the Gospel, they're seeing it acted out in a human relationship.

Prior to our courtship, I listened to a sermon series by John Piper on these verses in Ephesians 5 that had a huge impact on my understanding of the marriage relationship. I remember being stunned as I listened to Pastor Piper explain how God's purpose in marriage was so much greater than two individuals coming together: it was designed to point to the greater reality of the Gospel. As early as when God ordained the marriage relationship in Genesis, he had the future marriage between Jesus and his Bride, the Church, in mind.[1] When Scott and I got married and said our vows, our lives became a flesh and blood portrait of this solemn, spectacular reality.

All marriages are designed to be portraits of the Gospel. As wives, we have the marvelous privilege of daily displaying the Gospel before our children in the way we love and submit to our husbands. When we do this well, we glorify

God and offer a rich legacy to the next generation. When we do this poorly, we obscure God's main illustration of how he relates to his Church, and our children suffer as a result of the blurred image.

GOSPEL BLUEPRINTS

What does this look like, you might ask? In Ephesians 5, Paul addresses both the husband and the wife. He sets up parallel truths. First, he instructs wives to "submit to their own husbands, as to the Lord…as the church submits to Christ" (vv. 22, 24). In these verses, the wife is being compared to the Church. Next, the husband is to love his wife "as Christ loved the church and gave himself up for her" (v. 25). The husband is being compared to Christ.

Then, in verse 31, Paul refers to Genesis 2:24 where it says "Therefore a man shall leave his father and his mother and hold fast to his wife, and they shall become one flesh." He's referring to the institution of marriage, when God first introduced this idea that a man and woman would come together to start a brand-new home and family. By referencing the origin of marriage, Paul reminds the Ephesians that marriage and a godly form of a wife's submission to her husband was God's idea from the very beginning.

The Ephesian Christians thought they knew about marriage, but Paul wants to tell them something new—not new to God—but something very possibly new to their way of thinking. He says that marriage is a "profound mystery," and then he declares that "...it [marriage] refers to Christ and the church" (v. 32). Can you imagine their thoughts and questions as these truths began to sink in?

From the very beginning, God designed marriage to point to the relationship between Christ and the Church! From Genesis to Revelation, God has had a plan to use earthly marriages and the sexual identity of men and women (as established in Genesis) as a picture not just of his image in humanity, but of the Gospel. Revelation 19:7 joyously celebrates: "Let us rejoice and exult and give him the glory, for the marriage of the Lamb has come, and his Bride has made herself ready."

So, as husband and wife, Scott and I are actually acting out and painting a picture of the parallel (and more significant) roles of both Christ and his Church. We can embrace this reality in a way that adorns the Gospel or balk at it, distorting the glory of the full picture. Paul's instruction that wives submit to their husbands and that husbands love their wives takes on proper meaning and weight in light of this picture. How Scott and I live out these roles reflects what we believe about the Gospel.

Do we take the Gospel—the news that Jesus died on the cross for our sins—seriously? If so, then we will want to display that truth as accurately and as biblically as possible. Does it really matter whether I submit to and respect my husband? Yes, it does, in consequential ways. The Church submits to Christ, not the other way around; similarly, wives submit to their husbands, not the other way around. My attitude and response toward my husband reflect what I truly believe about the Church's relationship to Christ. This has practical implications for the way Scott and I set up our home and teach our children, and I want to mention just two of them here.

WORKING AT HOME

As Scott acts out his role of loving and serving me as Christ loves and serves the church, one thing he does is take responsibility for providing for the financial needs of our family. This doesn't mean that I won't ever work or earn money for the family (the Proverbs 31 woman is quite the productive lady!), but Scott sees himself as the primary bread-winner. This is his burden to bear before the Lord. Especially while our children are young, this releases me to be the primary caregiver and nurturer in their lives.

In Titus 2, Paul exhorts the older women to teach several important values to the younger women. One of those values is working at home. Just as we need to be taught to love our husbands and children, Paul also suggests that we need to be taught to work at home.

There is immense value to spending time in our homes and making them places of refuge and joy for our families.

Whether we stay home with our children full-time or not, we are supposed to take our work at home seriously. It's important to God, and it's important to our loved ones!

I think this also means that we need to think carefully about work outside of the home. As moms with small children, Titus 2 is clear about our priorities. Are we living out of those priorities, or is work outside of the home clouding them? If you work outside of the home, here are some questions to ask yourself: Where is my heart primarily–in my home or outside of it? What is my motivation to work outside of the home? Are my children struggling in any way because of my decision, directly or indirectly?

Some of you may wish you could stay home with your young children, but you don't know how to make that happen. It isn't easy to stay home in a culture that sets up its financial structures assuming that there will be two bread-winners, and even though I say this with tongue firmly planted in cheek, I could probably write a chapter titled "Loving My Children on a Budget." It's not as if things are getting any less expensive.

Scott and I live in New Jersey, a state with a reputation for exceptionally high property taxes and expenses. Many of our friends have walked through seasons of financial struggle when the wife has worked at least part-time to make ends meet. We feel a lot of sympathy for moms of young children who want to stay home but who just don't know how to make that happen.

If you are a stay-at-home mom, be thankful and purposeful with the gift of that circumstance. There are women who want to be home but can't during these precious early years. For all the challenges that I juggle at home, I'm so grateful that I don't have to balance my work there with regular work outside of the home. Not only is it a privilege to serve my children this way, but being home offers opportunities to serve neighbors and my church in ways that I couldn't if I were serving the needs of an employer.

BOYS TO MEN AND GIRLS TO WOMEN

As we consider and embrace Paul's teaching on loving our husbands and the Gospel portrait on display in our marriages, it should also motivate us to pass on biblical roles to the next generation. Biblical roles related to the distinction of being male and female are good and godly, and not only do we want to experience all that God has for us in them, but we also want our children to experience the grace that accompanies living according to God's design for sexuality. How do we do this? Like most things that we pass on to our children, instruction often takes place in the mundane activities of life. We ought to encourage our little ones when they're acting like little "men" and "women."

We know a couple in our church who are a great example of this kind of intentionality. They have three young adult children, a daughter and two sons. The husband plans one-on-one time with the boys, and the wife occasionally takes the boys out on individual dates; similarly, she spends one-on-one time with their daughter, and he occasionally takes their daughter out on dates. These contexts create purposeful opportunities for them to talk with each child about honoring God in their present and future friendships, in addition to casting vision for how to grow as men and women.

MOMS ON THEIR OWN—SORT OF

I'm sensitive to the fact that there might be moms reading this chapter who are on their own. Maybe you've never married, you're married to an unbelieving husband, or you're divorced or widowed. We live in a messy world, and our lives tell tales of its complexity. Paul writes about "the sufferings of this present time," and while we wait on this side of eternity for Christ to return, there will be suffering (Rom. 8:18). Being on your own as a Christian mom is tough. But you're not really alone. None of us are. Jesus promises, "And behold, I am with you always, to the end of the age" (Matt. 28:20). *Jesus himself* is actually with those who love and follow him.

If this is you, the best way you can love your children is still to pass on the Gospel to them. Yes, marriage is a picture that points to the Gospel, but the Gospel is the real thing, the ultimate reality. Even if you don't have a husband who is a picture of Christ giving up his life for the Church, you know Christ himself, the one who gave up his life for you, the Lamb who takes away the sins of the world.

In 2 Timothy 1:5, Paul encourages Timothy by reminding him of his family legacy of faith: "I am reminded of your sincere faith, a faith that dwelt first in your grandmother Lois and your mother Eunice and now, I am sure, dwells in you as well." In this passage, there is no mention of Timothy's father. Instead, Paul highlights the sincere faith of Timothy's grandmother and mother who faithfully and effectively passed the Gospel to the next generation.

Paul goes on, "But as for you, continue in what you have learned and have firmly believed, knowing from whom you have learned it and how from childhood you have been acquainted with the sacred writings, which are able to make you wise for salvation through faith in Christ Jesus" (2 Tim. 3:14-15). In these verses, Paul exhorts Timothy to continue in faith because of the example and teaching of his youth. If you do not have the support of a Christian husband, may these verses encourage you! God can use your life, example and teaching to lead your children to Jesus.

No matter what your story is, please consider what

Scripture teaches about marriage. Rather than allowing bitterness (about what we don't have) to take root in our hearts, let's point out Christian marriages that, though imperfect, represent the covenant relationship between Christ and the Church. Let's help our children understand biblical roles for men and women. And, let's commit to praying that our children and any future spouses will enjoy the good gift of marriages that celebrate the Gospel.

CHAPTER FOUR

Fearfully and Wonderfully Made

One day, a friend phoned me to see whether she could come over. She didn't say much, but it sounded as though she'd been crying. When she arrived, we put my two boys in strollers and started walking and talking as we wove our way through the neighborhood.

My husband and I have gotten to know and love this dear friend and her husband over the past couple of years. As newlyweds, one of the challenges they've faced in the leaving-and-cleaving process has been relating to her mother. As a single mom, her mother had high hopes and plans for her daughter. She had invested financially in her daughter's education, and she was very excited at her daughter's plans to attend medical school. When my friend's relationship with the Lord blossomed in college, some of those plans changed. Higher education was no longer her greatest goal, and graduate school took a backseat when she and her husband met and decided to get married.

As we walked, my friend confessed that she'd finally told her mom a secret that she'd been holding onto for awhile. She told her mom that she was pregnant, and this news didn't go over very well. Although her mom tried to sound happy, my friend told me that she was more aware of her mom's disappointment and sadness at the news. My friend said that in that moment, she sadly realized that her mother would prefer that she earn three Masters' degrees than raise three children.

When it comes to loving our children, the world throws many obstacles in our way. We live in a society that is far from child-friendly, and at times we need to love our children in the face of a barrage of negative press and public opinion. Even some family members and friends can say things that make us feel guilty for having children. Sometimes well-meaning folks may assert their opinions, saying that they think we're having children too soon, too close together or, for goodness' sake, just having too *many* of them!

Whether faced with warped societal values or dealing with those who take offense at our offspring, we have to come to grips with the fact that the world doesn't love our children, except maybe as a marketing target. We live in a culture that is largely against us in our parenting endeavor, *especially* if we seek to parent biblically. We cannot take our cues on loving our children from the world. Instead, in our pursuit to love our children biblically, let's take heart and be encouraged by what God has to say about the value and worth of children made in his image.

FEARFULLY AND WONDERFULLY MADE

God created the first man and the first woman, and he blessed them, saying, "Be fruitful and multiply and fill the earth and subdue it and have dominion" (Gen. 1:28). His first command to Adam and Eve was to "be fruitful and multiply and fill the earth." In other words, have kids! This was God's good plan and design, even before the Fall. "And God saw everything that he had made, and behold, it was very good" (Gen. 1:31). God didn't make man and then step back and think, "Oh, I made a big mistake." No. He called what he made "good." And it was good because he said it was good.

But after that first act of creation giving us Adam and Eve, who does the creating in every birth thereafter? Does God really have a hand in the conception of every child, or is it up to the man and woman who come together? We're going to look more closely at God's sovereignty in the next chapter, but for now, we need to recognize that what we believe about the Creator and his authority over creation powerfully influences what we think and believe about children.

In a culture that encourages family planning, even Christians can find themselves taking too much credit for conception or the lack of it. Yes, a husband and wife play a significant role in conceiving a child (by God's design), but I can name couples whose plans for their families haven't gone the way they intended. Some have tried for years and haven't been able to conceive; others thought they were doing everything possible to prevent a pregnancy, and found out they were expecting. This is what I consider the "God factor" in conception. How do our hearts react when God steps into our plans for childbearing and, by thwarting our best laid plans, reminds us that he is sovereign over the life of every human being?

King David doesn't just defend God's hand in creating and forming life—he celebrates it. Listen to his words of praise in Psalm 139:

> For you formed my inward parts;
> You knitted me together in my mother's womb.
> I praise you, for I am fearfully
> and wonderfully made.
> Wonderful are your works;
> My soul knows it very well.
> My frame was not hidden from you,
> When I was being made in secret,
> Intricately woven in the depths of the earth.
> Your eyes saw my unformed substance;
> In your book were written, every one of them,

the days that were formed for me,
When as yet there were none of them.

David acknowledges that "when as yet there were none of them," even before his days began, God had written all the days that were formed for him. God had a plan for his life, and it began in his mother's womb where God shaped and molded him in secret. The same God who made Adam and Eve in the Garden of Eden also formed and knit together David's body so that he was "fearfully and wonderfully made." This is the same God whose hands carefully craft each and every one of our children.

A HERITAGE, REWARD AND BLESSING

When I was talking with the friend I mentioned at the beginning of this chapter, my heart ached. Not only because she had heard words of discouragement and sadness from her mother, but because the news of a baby's coming birth should have been a great joy. Her mother, like many others in our society, saw this new life as a disruption to her daughter's purpose and overall mission in life.

By comparison, in God's Word, children are described as a "heritage," "reward" and "blessing":

Behold, children are a *heritage* from the LORD,
the fruit of the womb a *reward*.
Like arrows in the hand of a warrior
are the children of one's youth.
Blessed is the man who fills his

quiver with them!"
(Psalm 127:3-5, emphasis mine)

"Heritage," "reward" and "blessing" are not words of dishonor, but honor. Even though the strident voices of our culture may characterize children as a hindrance or burden, God calls them a blessing.

In the first chapter of Luke, the angel Gabriel announces to Zechariah that his barren wife Elizabeth will bear a son. He says, "And you will have joy and gladness, and many will rejoice at his birth." What a beautiful response this is to God's work creating and bringing life into being! I want my heart to have the same response of joy and gladness, rejoicing over God's gift of children, whether my own or the children of others.

A BATTLE OF THE HEART

Sometimes our struggle to believe God's Word about our children doesn't come from an external attack by the world and its systems of thought. Often, it's a battle raging inside our own hearts. Even when we acknowledge God's hand in creating our children, it can be hard to embrace this truth when doing so challenges our expectations and comfort. I want to address two groups of moms that might be fighting this battle. First, I want to encourage moms who are wrestling with God and struggling to love their children because of a child's mental, emotional or physical limitations. Next, there may be moms who are having a hard time loving their children because they've come to see their children as more of a burden than a blessing.

Perhaps you're reading this chapter and you feel gripped by very real hurt, disappointment or discouragement because when you look at your son or daughter, you see a mental, physical or emotional challenge, and you don't understand how or why God could allow—let alone ordain—this trial in your child's life. Maybe you're feeling exhausted, overwhelmed or even defeated, and you're simply not sure how to honor God in this trial. If this is you, I want to come alongside of you in your struggle. I pray that something in this book would encourage and strengthen your faith as you seek to love your child. Isaiah 30:18 says that "the LORD waits to be gracious to you... blessed are all those who wait for him."

If it's hard for you to trust God's goodness in this circumstance, and if this is one of the roots of your struggle to love your child, please wait for God, and don't give up the fight to experience his grace as you depend on him. There is no other Rock in whom you can trust; all others will fail you.

We live in a world that, although created good, is now under judgment and marred by sin in profound ways. We do not live in the beautiful Garden of Eden but in the fallen and sin-stained world of Genesis 3. Nevertheless, despite man's sinful, fallen state, God remains good, and his purposes prevail over sin and death. Jesus Christ died on the cross to set us free from the law of sin and death. He is our hope in our fight against the bitterness, anxiety, fear and anger in our own hearts. He is our hope for forgiveness, peace, joy and gratitude. Despite the horrible consequences of disease and death and their impact even on Christians and their children, we look back to the cross where death was defeated, and we look forward to heaven where all things, including disease and infirmity, will be reversed and made right again.

In the meantime, all people are still God's image-bearers. Though distorted or distressed, the Bible teaches that there is value to all human life because it is God's creation and bears his mark. The world doesn't value children that way. Some doctors go so far as to recommend and encourage an abortion if a deformity seems likely, based on prenatal tests. Although our culture and society exalt mental prowess, physical beauty and emotional stability, the Lord does not look at the outward appearance but at the heart. He is the Author of each individual life, and, as moms, we need to remind ourselves that he who formed our children is good and faithful, and he has a plan for each child's life.

BURDEN OR BLESSING?

Even though we've heard the words, we don't always live

like our children are "fearfully and wonderfully made" when we're in the middle of hard mothering tasks. I think that all of us can get caught in the trap of habitually seeing our children as a burden rather than a blessing. This can happen for a number of reasons.

Mothering moments can reveal our hearts. When my infant son started spraying pee all over the restaurant bathroom while I changed his diaper, then giggled as I frantically wiped down the walls and floor with baby wipes, was I marveling at God's good design? As I washed off this child's feet in the sink, praying that no stranger would walk through the door and see my makeshift bathtub, I wanted to cry. Everything in me yelled, "I just can't do this!"

It wasn't funny to me at that precise moment. But, graciously, the Lord reminded me that this would be one of the things that I would laugh at in the days to come. I could choose to cry, or I could start laughing right then and there. What would it be? This time I decided to laugh, and the story is now one that my kids love to hear over and over again.

But sometimes the tasks and duties of caring for small children become draining over the long haul, and it's easy to succumb to the temptation to resent the little ones whom we perceive as demanding our time and attention. We forget to see them as blessings because we're more aware of the work they add to our lives.

Seeing children as burdens instead of blessings can also be a temptation when we find ourselves caught in a trap of comparing our sons or daughters to other children. We wish they would perform better in school or on the athletic field, or be more enthusiastic, act less shy or be more popular. Some of us would settle for "normal," (whatever that is). "If only Peter were more like Paul or Susie were more like Sarah," we think. Maybe we're caught in a trap of comparing ourselves to other moms, not just admiring another with thanks for a good example, but dying by degrees as we compare our perceived (or glaringly real) gaps in gifting, knowledge, skill or even diligence in parenting.

Maybe your struggle has more to do with your child's individuality. He or she "ticks" differently than you do, and it bugs you! There are personality traits that bother or even embarrass you when other people are present. Your child's habits annoy you.

The end result is the same in all of these cases. When our children start to feel like burdens that we have to endure, we're robbed of the joy of loving them as the unique individuals God designed them to be, and they are robbed of the joy of being loved as gifts. So how do we fight for the joy of seeing each child as a gift?

SPEAKING TRUTH

This fight requires us to change who talks and who listens

inside our heads. As Martyn Lloyd-Jones says in his excellent book *Spiritual Depression*:

> I say that we must talk to ourselves instead of allowing 'our selves' to talk to us! ... The main art in the matter of spiritual living is to know how to handle yourself. You have to take yourself in hand, you have to address yourself, preach to yourself, question yourself. You must say to your soul: 'Why art thou cast down'—what business have you to be disquieted? You must turn on yourself, upbraid yourself, condemn yourself, exhort yourself, and say to yourself: 'Hope thou in God'—instead of muttering in this depressed, unhappy way. And then you must go on to remind yourself of God, Who God is, and what God is and what God has done, and what God is about.[2]

When we're tempted to believe lies about God or our children or ourselves, we need to fight those lies with the truth of God's Word. What helps you "take yourself in hand"? Is it index cards with Bible verses on them that hang above your kitchen sink or on your bathroom mirror? Do you play a worship CD and start singing the lyrics? Do you ever call a trusted friend and ask her to pray for you?

When society criticizes God's handiwork, we're tempted to question God's goodness, and we can start to believe that our children are more of a burden than a blessing. We need to take captive these lying thoughts and speak truth to ourselves: This child is a blessing. This child is a good gift from God to our family. My blessing. Our gift. We can ask God to give us insight into the people he's made our children to be and ask him to grow gratitude in our hearts for each particular child. By God's grace, we can also verbally express our love for our child: "I'm so glad you were born. I'm so glad God made you just the way he did." And we can really mean it when we do. How seldom do we speak the good truth we could to those who need it most? It usually costs us very little (besides our pride) to do so.

JESUS IN JUDEA

I can imagine Jesus sitting on a hillside, surrounded by local farmers and fishermen and villagers who are waiting with bated breath to hear the next words he will speak—something eloquent and profound, words that will confound their leaders and give meaning to their lives. Then, onto the scene comes a stream of parents, toddlers on their shoulders and young children trotting alongside them. The vigilant disciples run forward, putting their hands up and crying, "No! Stop! The Teacher is busy!"

Like so many today who see children as interfering with what in their minds is truly important (not always, but often selfish ambitions and goals), the disciples viewed these children as interfering with Jesus' ministry. Once again, Jesus says something that challenges our understanding of the Kingdom of God. The Good Shepherd, who gently leads those with young, interrupts his zealous, short-sighted disciples: "Let the little children come to me and do not hinder them, for to such belongs the kingdom of heaven" (Matt. 19:14).

We might live in a culture that is critical of children, but our Lord Jesus welcomes them. Some days, we might even believe that we're too busy for the interruptions that children bring to us. But Jesus never says that he is too busy for children.

As moms, it's our privilege to bring our children to Jesus. He might not lay his flesh-and-blood hands on them and pray for them; but, nevertheless, the same Jesus who fearfully and wonderfully made our children invites us to bring them to him in prayer, to show them his love and his ways, and to tell them about him. As we proclaim the Gospel to them, one day, Lord-willing, they will come to know him as their Savior.

CHAPTER FIVE

What Does Doctrine Have to Do with Being a Mom?

One morning, I drove two-year-old John Luke and four-year-old Elijah to my friend Shana's house so our kids could play and we could catch up. At the time, Shana had two little ones and a baby on the way. Let me help you picture the scene. A heart-to-heart conversation was interrupted by John Luke wetting the toy dust broom in the dog's water bowl to clean the hardwood floor. From there, we navigated our conversation around various potty breaks, sibling conflicts and juice requests. Shana handled the interruptions amazingly well.

The best part, though, was toward the end of our time together. As we were praying, her daughter walked in with a broken toy. Opening her eyes to address the situation, Shana saw what was in her daughter's hand. "It's a piece of a maraca!" We jumped up, ran to the toy room and began picking up the tiny stones that had once filled the instrument before one of the smaller children decided to taste one. Prayer ended quickly.

That morning with Shana was pretty funny, but I don't always drive away laughing. As a mom with young children, things like this happen all the time. Conversations are interrupted, agendas wander off course and relational expectations frequently go unmet. What do I do when things like this happen and my plans are thwarted?

As much as I'd rather not admit it, more often than not I start feeling frustrated and sorry for myself. Sometimes it seems as though it's not even worth going out at all to be with other moms and kids because I'm afraid my desire for heart-level conversation will be disappointed. It's so easy for me to slip into the false thinking that says, "It's all about me," and to forget that God has a greater purpose in mind than my comfort during this season of mothering my young ones.

Slowly, the Lord is teaching me to shift my perspective in these moments. The title of this chapter is "What Does Doctrine Have to Do With Being a Mom?" Well, good doctrine has everything to do with earthy, everyday motherhood! Doctrine is about living the life God intends for us, the way He intends it. Whether it's in mundane mornings spent with other moms and kids or when we're wrestling with God's wisdom and design on a grander scale, we need to know what the Bible teaches in order to live in a God-glorifying way with our kids.

EXPLORING GOD'S SOVEREIGNTY

Simply put, Bible doctrines are the teachings of Scripture, and one doctrine that is growing increasingly precious to me as a mom of young children is the doctrine of God's sovereignty. From cover to cover, the Bible teaches that God is sovereign. But what does this word mean?

When I look up "sovereign" in Webster's dictionary, I find this definition of the noun: "One who possesses supreme authority, especially a person...in whom the supreme power of the state is vested."[3] By that definition, a sovereign is a kind of person. When the word is used as an adjective to describe someone, some of those definitions include, "Exercising or possessing supreme jurisdiction or power," "free, independent, and in no way limited by external authority or influence," and "possessing supreme excellence of greatness." So, when we talk about God being sovereign, we're referring to his excellent greatness, his supreme authority and power, and the reality that he acts independent of any other authority. Is this close to what Scripture has in mind?

In his first letter to Timothy, Paul refers to God as the "blessed and only Sovereign, the King of kings and Lord of lords" (1 Tim. 6:15). In this one verse, Paul uses three political labels to identify God's authority in exclusive and preeminent terms. God is the only Sovereign, he is King of kings, and he is Lord of lords. As Sovereign, God is the only being in the universe with complete and final authority over all things. As King of kings, God is above any earthly king crowned by the nations (or who crowns himself), and as King of the universe, God has complete control over all that he has created. Finally, God is Lord of lords, higher than any authority established by mankind.

Part of being a Christian is confessing that "Jesus is Lord," (Rom. 10:9), and we're told in Philippians that one day "every tongue" will "confess that Jesus Christ is Lord, to the glory of God the Father" (Phil. 2:11). In this passage, God the Father exalts Jesus the Son as Lord over all.

God can do whatever he wants, whenever he wants, however he wants and to whomever he wants. In his book *Trusting God: Even When Life Hurts*, Jerry Bridges explains how this kind of power would be a frightening thing if God did not also reveal himself to be completely wise and loving. We don't need to be frightened because his power as Sovereign is matched by perfect wisdom and love. Precisely because God is also wise and loving, not only is he *able* to anything, but we can trust him to do that which is *best* at all times.

When King David declares that "the lines have fallen for

me in pleasant places," he's not just saying that he likes a particular plot of land that he inherited (Ps. 16:5). The application goes further and deeper. God sets many kinds of boundaries on our lives, and when we embrace those boundaries, we find that they are good.

When I was six years old, I watched gymnast Mary Lou Retton score a 10.0 in the 1984 Olympics and I dreamed of being a star gymnast someday. Not only did I never become an Olympic gymnast, but I have kyphoscoliosis, a congenital back disorder that didn't even allow me to try my hand at gymnastics as a girl. It wasn't safe. Was God somehow being unkind by setting this very real boundary on my life?

Or, when I look back at my schooling and think about all the career possibilities that seemed to be in front of me, should I be disappointed that I pursued one path and not another one? Did I miss something there? What about marriage? Did I marry "Mr. Right," or someone less than that?

It's true that boundary lines "have fallen for me." There are choices and decisions that I can't undo. But, when I look around at all that God has done and brought to pass in my life, I'm amazed by how good and right the lines he has set for me really are. That doesn't mean I don't ever have questions about difficulties or suffering in my own life or the lives of others, but it does mean that there is a general sense of the rightness of God's works that fosters trust in the future.

Far from being a stifling doctrine, a right understanding of God's sovereignty can transform our view of God and cause us to delight in and worship him all the more. Your season of motherhood might be different than mine or someone else's, but when it comes to everyday living, can you really live as though you believe that God is sovereign over all things, even your given season and circumstances?

In this chapter, I want to focus on two amazing implications of God's sovereignty when it's specifically applied to motherhood. First, God chose me to be the mother of my children. Second, God chose my children for me in particular. Embracing these truths will strengthen our faith, encourage our hearts and better equip us to love our children in daily life, whatever the future holds for us.

GOD CHOSE ME TO BE THE MOTHER OF MY CHILDREN

Have you ever taken the time to ponder this thought? Of all the women who've ever lived, throughout all of human history, God could have picked anyone to be the mother of your children. But he chose you. Not because there's anything remarkable about you, but because it was the best plan to bring about his purposes in your life and in the lives of your children. With your particular set of strengths, weaknesses and idiosyncrasies, God chose you to be the mother of your children.

I love reading the genealogy of Jesus Christ in the first chapter of the Gospel of Matthew. It's not at all what one would expect to find in a narrative account in the Bible. If it had been up to me, Jesus' ancestors would have been purely Jewish, blameless men and women commended by God as people of impeccable character and faith. Thankfully, God doesn't do things the way I would. Included in the list of Jesus' ancestors are Tamar, Rahab, Ruth and Bathsheba. These were unlikely women, given conventional wisdom, but their selection in Jesus' lineage and their inclusion in the genealogical list is no accident. Rather, their stories display God's sovereignty and magnify his love for all peoples, apart from ethnicity or background.

First, let's consider Tamar. Genesis 38 tells the story of how Judah, one of Jacob's twelve sons, took Tamar to be the wife of his firstborn son, Er. But Er was "wicked in the sight of the LORD, and the LORD put him to death" (v. 7). After waiting several years for a kinsman-redeemer, a man in the family who would raise up an heir for Er, Tamar took matters into her own hands. When she heard that Judah, her father-in-law, was in town, she took off her widow's garments and dressed as a prostitute; Judah took her sexually, and she conceived a child. Later, when Judah was informed of Tamar's pregnancy, he assumed that she was guilty and ordered that she be burned. However, when she proved that Judah was the father of the twins in her womb, he confessed that she was more righteous than he was. By God's sovereign wisdom, Tamar's son Perez, by Judah, was included in the lineage of Jesus.

What about Rahab? Identified as a prostitute in the city of Jericho, she hid two Israelite spies and was rewarded with her life when her city was destroyed. The author of Hebrews identifies her as a woman of notable faith: "By faith Rahab the prostitute did not perish with those who were disobedient, because she had given a friendly welcome to the spies" (Heb. 11:31). Despite her former life in the city of Jericho, she acted in faith and receives biblical commendation for choosing to fear the God of the Hebrews. Matthew gives us another hint that a radical change took place in Rahab's life. By Salmon, she became the mother of Boaz. Scripture describes Boaz as a "worthy man" (Ruth 2:1), and Boaz shows himself to be both generous and godly. I can only guess that God did a great work in Rahab's life so that she would be equipped to raise such a son.

Now, let's look at the life of Ruth. Elimelech was an Israelite from Judah who took his wife Naomi and two sons to live in Moab during a severe famine. Although the Israelites were commanded not to marry Moabites, both of the sons, Mahlon and Chilion, married Moabite women. Ruth was one of those women. When Elimelech, Mahlon and Chilion died, Naomi decided to return to Judah, and her tearful daughter-in-law, Ruth, insisted she go with her: "Where you go I will go, and where you lodge I will lodge. Your people shall be my people, and your God my God" (Ruth 1:16). Again, God takes an unlikely candidate and sovereignly weaves a tale of grace. A beautiful story covered with God's fingerprints unfolds, and Ruth marries Boaz and conceives Obed, becoming the great-grand-mother of King David, a critical covenant turning-point in the genealogy of Jesus Christ.

Finally, Matthew tells us that "David was the father of Solomon by the wife of Uriah" (Matt. 1:6). Yes, David commits adultery with Uriah's wife, Bathsheba, and through grievous intrigue, he brings her into his home as his wife. Can you put yourself in Bathsheba's shoes? First, the king uses her, he murders her husband and, finally, the baby she carries full-term dies. Where is God when all of this happens? God is right there.

And he works good out of the sinful details of this horrif-ic story. God is sovereign in the life of Bathsheba, and he is working for the sovereign good of all of his people. For out of the unlikely union of David and Bathsheba, another son is born, Solomon—also known as Jedidiah, meaning "beloved of the LORD"—who is included in the kingly lineage of Jesus Christ. God had a plan for Bathsheba and a plan for her son Solomon, but he was also working out his ultimate plan of redemption for mankind. I doubt that any of this seemed evident or likely at the time.

THAT THEY SHOULD SEEK GOD

God took four unlikely women and included them in the lineage of his only Son. Tamar conceived by deception, Rahab had a more than questionable past, Ruth was a non-Jew, and Bathsheba was caught in a web of adultery. Yet God, in his sovereignty, chose each of these women to be part of his plan to redeem mankind.

Let's pause and consider our own redemption stories. What did it take for God to bring you into his family? What trials and challenges did you have to walk through before you surrendered your heart to him? How far did you have to travel to hear the Gospel? Maybe you feel like you're an unlikely candidate for salvation. You might wonder about your qualifications as a mother and feel inadequate to parent the children he has given you, yet God chose you to be their mother. Why?

I believe that Paul's preaching to non-believers in Athens early in the life of the Church provides us with an important clue that helps answer this question. In Acts 17, Paul tells the Athenians about the sovereign God who "made from one man every nation of mankind to live on all the face of the earth, having determined allotted periods and the boundaries of their dwelling place, that they should seek God, in the hope that they might feel their way toward him and find him" (vv. 26-27). God has determined "allotted periods" (when a person is born and lives) and the "boundaries of their dwelling place" (where and with whom that person lives) so that people "should seek God, in the hope that they might feel their way toward him and find him."

As a Christian, God has made you the mother of your children to position them to hear the Gospel and find him. You may not proclaim the Gospel perfectly to them, and you are not the only means of access to Gospel truth, but if you confess the Lord and he has brought you from death to life by his Spirit, he has blessed your children with a Christian mother. They are well-positioned to come to know him.

This should give you confidence that despite your very real weaknesses, God has a great and specific purpose for you being the mother of your children, and he will be faithful to fulfill his purpose and plan both for your life and the lives of any children with whom he blesses you.

GOD CHOSE THESE CHILDREN FOR ME

If God sovereignly orchestrated circumstances for me to be the mother of my children in particular, then he also sovereignly arranged for my children to be mine. The difference isn't just a difference of wording; it's one of perspective. I believe that one of God's primary purposes in giving them to me is my sanctification.

One of my favorite verses for applying God's sovereignty is Romans 8:28-29: "And we know that for those who love God all things work together for the good, for those who are called according to his purpose. For those whom he foreknew he also predestined to be conformed to the image of his Son." This is a glorious, hope-filled promise for believers. If we love God, we're invited to embrace the truth these verses proclaim, that "all things work together for good." And what is that good? That we might be conformed to the image of his Son. The theological name for this kind of conforming is called "sanctification."

As mothers, the "all things" includes the sometimes messy process of raising our children. Our relationship with each child in our family is part of God's plan to make us more like Jesus. No child is identical to another, and God knit each one together as a unique individual with his or her own gifts, abilities, strengths, weaknesses and personalities. Then, he placed this child in our homes for us to love, care for and nurture. Even if it's hard, it's all part of God's beautiful design.

At the beginning of this chapter, I shared the story about my visit with my friend Shana. It helps me to step back and consider God's sovereignty in the big picture so that I can remember that he's also very much involved in the everyday details of life. On a regular basis, God presents us with opportunities to set aside our own plans, ambitions, never-ending lists and desires to serve our children.

So, when my adult conversations are interrupted by the needs of my child, it's not an accident, but an opportunity. Maybe it's an opportunity to realize that my child's need is greater than my own desire to finish a conversation, and God is inviting me to serve and nurture my child in that moment. Perhaps it's an opportunity for me to train my child in learning patience, teaching him to wait for me to finish my conversation before his need is met. Along the way, I'm learning to put to death my own selfishness and to consider the needs of another.

This doesn't work in only one direction. God uses a child to help us see when we want and crave something more than obedience to him, and he uses us to help our children understand when they crave something more than obedience to God. God is often at work for our mutual sanctification.

THE FRUIT OF EMBRACING GOD'S SOVEREIGNTY

God chose us to be the mothers of our particular children, and he chose these very same children for us. Our inadequacies, failures and weaknesses as moms only further highlight the Lord's adequacy, faithfulness and great strength to fulfill his purposes. He does have a plan that's grander than ours, and it's a plan of redemption and sanctification, and he cannot be thwarted in carrying it out.

Embracing the doctrine of God's sovereignty can produce wonderful fruit in a mother's heart. It humbles us and lifts our eyes to the only Sovereign, King of kings and Lord of lords. It bolsters our faith when we're faced with trials—even seemingly mundane trials—like having prayers interrupted by a broken toy, or more life-altering trials, like the death of a child or the sudden, unexpected reality of single parenthood. When life circumstances remind us that we're not in control, however much we act as if we are, God's hand in our lives reminds us that he is always acting, always watching and always in control.

Learning to commit both the present and future details of our children's lives to the Lord can lead to contentment, peace and joy. We can have contentment, accepting and even celebrating the boundary lines that God sets for their lives, believing that he is in control and working for all of our good in ways that we can't even see or understand. We can have peace, knowing that nothing is going to happen to our children apart from God's knowledge, and nothing can happen that is somehow outside of his sphere of power. Finally, we can have joy, trusting in the goodness of our heavenly Father who cares more about our joy and our children's joy than we do—ultimately for his glory and the sake of his holy name.

CHAPTER SIX

The Greatest Hindrance to Loving My Children

What is the greatest hindrance to loving my children? The simple answer is that I am. I am the greatest hindrance to loving my children.

It's tempting to think that the world is my greatest enemy in this fight to love my own flesh and blood. True, the world tries to entice, tempt and claim their hearts. But in my home, worldly influences aren't usually the main obstacle to faithful parenting. I'm the enemy at the gate— inside the gate, in fact! My sinful heart rebels against selfless love. This reality illustrates another important Bible doctrine, the doctrine of original sin.

In the Garden of Eden, our first human mother, Eve, believed Satan's lies, doubted God's words, gave in to her own sinful craving and disobeyed God's command. Adam followed right on her heels. Not only do we, her daughters, now live in a fallen world, but we've inherited the same sinful nature through Adam's sin. Only by trusting in Jesus' atoning work on the cross can we be forgiven and set free from the law of sin and death that now exists as a consequence of Adam and Eve's initial disobedience.

Through faith in Christ, we're no longer bound by the law and its demands, but God gives us new hearts that can love him and worship him and live for Him—not things rebellious human hearts are ever inclined to do naturally. In Romans 7, Paul is clear about the ongoing conflict between our desire to do what is right and our remaining, indwelling sin. This battle for holiness will continue until we're in heaven with the Lord.

Thankfully, we're not left alone in this fight. In Romans 8, Paul goes on to describe the work of the Holy Spirit in the life of every believer: "For if you live according to the flesh you will die, but if by the Spirit you put to death the deeds of the body, you will live. For all who are led by the Spirit of God are sons of God" (vv. 13-14). When we're adopted as God's children, the Holy Spirit comes to live inside of us. He helps, encourages, convicts, counsels and reminds us of God's truth. By the Spirit's power, we are no longer bound by our sin but free to live the lives Christ died for us to live.

Let's pause for a moment. We're going to talk about sin

in this chapter—our sin—and any time we do that, we can be faced with a number of temptations. Instead of feeling condemned by our sinful tendencies, though, let's allow the Holy Spirit to convict us of sin and point us to Gospel hope. First Corinthians 10:13 says, "No temptation has overtaken you that is not common to man," and all of the sins that we're going to address are quite common to mothers. The same verse goes on to say that "God is faithful, and he will not let you be tempted beyond your ability, but with the temptation he will also provide the way of escape, that you may be able to endure it."

Our God is a faithful God, and he doesn't want us to be stuck in or feel paralyzed by our sin as we repent of it. As we recognize, acknowledge and confess the areas in which we are prone to temptation as moms, it grows easier to discern when we are being tempted, as well as to see the promised "way of escape." Ultimately, we can take comfort in knowing that if we're trusting Christ for salvation, then the sins we battle are also sins for which Jesus already died.

As we consider the following points, instead of focusing on our failures and striving to overcome them in our own strength, let's look to and lean on Jesus. When we're in the middle of a tense moment with a child and the Spirit brings our own sin to light, instead of being surprised or discouraged by it, we ought to thank God for helping us to see what's really at stake, humble ourselves and ask for grace to change. God isn't surprised by our sin. He knows all about it, and he will work his plan to make us more like Jesus in spite of it.

God has purposes for us and for our children, purposes that are bigger than our own plans and desires. Sanctification is often uncomfortable, coming by means we wouldn't likely choose for ourselves. But it's good discipline. It ultimately results in the glorious end of becoming more like Christ and, therefore, brings greater glory to God.

There's one more thing to say here. In a parent-child relationship, two hearts are involved: the parent's and the child's. Disciplining and training our children, the "little sinners" in our homes, is an important part of loving our children, too. That's why we'll address that topic in the next chapter. However, in looking at our own "big sinner" hearts, let's start where Jesus starts—by looking at the logs in our own eyes.

Your sin struggles might look a bit different from mine, but I hope that the Lord will use my weaknesses and temptations to point you to the same Savior and Gospel. Some of the sins that I am most painfully aware of when it comes to parenting my children are the sins of a judgmental spirit, selfishness and fear.

JUDGMENTAL SPIRIT

Talking with a friend about some of the challenges of motherhood, I made a comment concerning my children, the little sinners in my home. Gently, she reminded me of the big sinner in the house (me!). She was right. How easy it is to see my children's sin and to forget my own sin! It's hard to miss the grabbing and shoving and crying that comes with conflict among them some days. It's much easier to overlook my own idolatrous cravings for a quiet home.

Or, consider this scenario: My poor planning leads to a rush out the door, with the added threat of "or we'll be late!" Then my anger and impatience kick in when my son dawdles while putting on his shoes. My son may or may not be sinning when he is slow that way, but I'm giving in to sinful anger when I react and speak harshly to him. It's sobering to think that Christ died for sins like that.

Perhaps my sin isn't as obvious, but it's just as serious—likely worse and more culpable—than my child's. When I'm looking at my children's sins under a microscope but I'm blind to my own, there's a pretty good chance that I'm being ruled by a judgmental spirit. Jesus doesn't beat around the bush when it comes to judging others, and his words in Matthew 7:4-5 strike a chord with me: "...how can you say to your brother, 'Let me take the speck out of your eye,' when there is the log in your own eye? You hypocrite, first take the log out of your own eye, and then you will see clearly to take the speck out of your brother's eye."

Biblically, parents are instructed to discipline and train their children in the way they should go, and children are commanded to honor and obey their parents according to the authority God has given (Prov. 22:6 and Eph. 6:1-2). Nevertheless, as parents, we're not in a position of authority in order to lord over our children, but rather, our position is to lead them to the Gospel, speaking truth in love. If we're ever going to be able to help them with their sins and point them to a Savior, we must come to grips with the fact that we, too, are sinners. In fact, we've lived longer and sinned more than they have!

In other words, I have to acknowledge that, yes, there's a speck in my child's eye, but there's often quite a log in my own. If I understand Jesus correctly, I have to take out my own log before I'm ready to help my child with the speck in his eye. Believing this truth produces a kind of humility that lets me come alongside my child and really mean it when I say, "I'm just like you, I'm for you, and I want to help you fight the sin in your heart."

A humble heart asks questions without making assumptions, believes and thinks the best (unless proven otherwise), and seeks the good of the other. This is the kind of heart we want to have when we address sin in our children.

SELFISHNESS

If we're ever going to be able to fight sin effectively, we need to learn to recognize it and call it by its true name. This is true of selfishness. As human beings, we are naturally selfish. We think, plan and crave from the perspective of self. This comes so naturally that we often don't realize we're indulging this sin. Paul exhorts us in the second chapter of Philippians, "...in humility count others more significant than yourselves. Let each of you look not only to his own interests, but also to the interests of others" (vv. 3-4). We can only become people who "count others more significant" if we're transformed by the Gospel and value them differently as a result, and we can only love our children biblically if we become moms who count our children more significant than ourselves.

Although he was God, Jesus Christ humbled himself, "taking the form of a servant" and "becoming obedient to the point of death, even death on a cross" (Phil. 2:7-8). He poured out his life in service to others. As Mark 10:45 says, "For even the Son of Man came not to be served but to serve, and to give his life as a ransom for many." Christ's humble, sacrificial service, even to the point of death, assured our hope for salvation. As moms who are called to pour out our lives to serve our children, this example is also a beautiful picture of what our lives are to be like.

Changing diapers and doing laundry and cleaning behind the ears might seem humbling to you, but think of the one who washed the grimy feet of his disciples. Not many mommy tasks are glorious, but as we daily pour out our lives—our time, our energy and even our bodies—to serve our children, we "count [them] more significant" than ourselves. The call to motherhood is an invitation to serve, but so often selfishness gets in the way, and the person I want to serve the most is me, not someone else.

For example, if I sinfully had my way, our home would be quiet all the time and there would be no conflict. None at all. That doesn't sound so bad, does it? But, as my three boys play together (plus a sister now), the volume level in our home has only increased over the years, as well as the number and frequency of their conflicts. In these moments, how does my heart respond when my private utopia can't be realized?

Being noisy is not inherently sinful. What's a quiet home with children? Boring! So, in my craving for perpetual silence, not only do I want something that's unrealistic, but it's probably not best for anyone. Is it really ideal for little boys to sit still and color all day at the table? No, they are designed to be full of energy and life. God gave them things to do to learn to become men, and a lot of those things involve noise and mess.

So what's going on? My heart craves something that God never promised, a life of ease and comfort in which everything goes my way, all the time, everyone's happy and we all get along. Perfectly. All my ducks are now in a row. This is when the "it's all about me" syndrome displaces what could be a godly desire for decent order. If it were quiet all the time, I could daydream and think my own thoughts without interruption. If there were no conflict, I could go about my day crossing off the tasks on my to-do list and maybe even sneak in some downtime at the end of the day to do things I want to do, like watch a movie or curl up with a good book.

It's not that it's wrong to cross items off my list or to relax at the end of a tiring day. But, when I start getting angry because things aren't going my way, whether my children are sinning or not, it's a good indicator that I want something too much and that I'm being driven by a sinful, selfish desire, one that's all out of order and proportion to real needs and legitimate desires.

There are times when my craving for peace and quiet becomes very strong, yet I can't escape from a situation involving one or more of my children. My angry heart wants to enter the ring and fight for my "right" to a quiet home. In that moment, I need God's help to fight my selfishness instead. If I give in to my selfish heart and address the situation with resentment, the fruit will be anger and impatience. What they need from me is something very different: a gentle answer, a patient word, timely instruction, care, discipline or prayer.

Let me offer an example: when I was expecting our third son, Silas, it was easy for me to regard my *need* for an afternoon nap as a *right*, a God-ordained one, written in the *Book of Pregnant Mommy Rights*. By God's grace, circumstances usually worked out nicely and I could lie down for at least twenty or thirty minutes each day. Even if my older children didn't sleep, they would rest or read in their bedroom. Nevertheless, there were days when I'd just be drifting off to sleep and I'd hear a little voice calling me, "Mommy, I need to use the potty..." In that moment, my child wasn't acting sinfully. But I wanted a nap, and his sweet voice was keeping me from my perceived right. Instead of affection for my son, I'd find myself flooded with impatience and anger.

It's at those times—when my flesh wants to lead—that I need the Holy Spirit to lead me instead. Remember, the flesh, our natural tendency to sin, leads us to death, and the Spirit leads us to life. It amazes me how something as small as a nap can bring out my sin, yet that's exactly how selfish I am. It doesn't take much pressure to reveal it or provoke me to anger. In those tempting naptime moments, I asked God to help me not give in to my emotions and trust him, fighting to believe that he really would give me all I needed to make it through the rest of the day. The Lord knew that some days I needed my heart to be adjusted more than I needed a nap.

There are also times when my sinfulness reacts to the reality of a sin on the part of one or all of my children. When they sin (and not necessarily against me), I need God's help not to take it personally, but instead, to see that specific sin as primarily against God. Only then can I help my son or daughter reconcile not only with me or a sibling, but with God. I've had to ask my son to wait in his room while I confessed my anger and cried out for God to give me patience and grace. At other times, I've felt over-whelmed by my own lack of wisdom and I've phoned my husband to ask him to pray for and counsel me. And there was one day when I fell to the kitchen floor feeling totally overwhelmed, begging God to be strong in my weakness. I probably need to do that more often than I do.

James 4:6 reminds believers that God opposes pride, but "gives grace to the humble." This verse exhorts us to resist selfishness and embrace humility. Why humility? It pleas-es God. As we set aside our own interests to serve our chil-dren, God promises to give us grace to do so.

FEAR

Newly pregnant with my first baby, I stood by an airport window as my husband boarded a plane for a business trip to China. He was going to be gone for ten days, and for the first time it dawned on me that if his plane crashed or something happened to him overseas, I would be a single mom. What if my husband never came home? What would it be like to raise a child on my own? What if my child never knew his father?

Then, there was the fear in my heart that moment when Scott and I noticed three-year-old Elijah at the top of the ladder to a tree house (a really cool one), making his way toward a wooden bridge about twenty feet off the ground. I stood at the bottom as our friend calmly talked our son back down the ladder. Elijah made it to the ground with a huge grin on his face, unaware of the danger.

What about when John Luke, as a toddler, wandered away and got lost at a large state park beach in South Carolina? Sunbathers were mobilized to search, park rangers closed the front entrance and Scott scoured the water. After ten harrowing minutes, a stranger found our son wandering between sand dunes.

In all of these situations, my heart was pounding. Fear. I was a desperate mama crying out to God for help. But God's eyes were on my children the whole time. Despite my fears, these situations were opportunities to trust God my Father, who loves and cares about my children even more than I do and who alone numbers and orders their days. Apart from his permission, nothing evil will ever touch them. I can cling to my God who has both my best interests and the best interests of my children at heart.

But it's hard. Fear is multi-faceted.

I'm also prone to be fearful when it comes to finances. Despite my fear in this area, time and time again, I've experienced God's faithfulness to our family. I can confidently tell my children how God has provided not only for their needs (through gifts of diapers and second-hand clothes), but even for their desires. Once, Elijah really wanted a toy space shuttle for Christmas, but we couldn't find one in a store. Later, we spotted one in a giveaway pile at our church.

Fear doesn't only come into play when I'm concerned about my child's physical safety or our family's financial circumstances, though. Fear can also drive my concerns about what other people think (or don't think) about either my children or my parenting. I can be fearful for my children's future. And I can be fearful when I start comparing one child to his brother, or to someone else's child.

Is fear sinful? If I am fearful, it reveals something about what I functionally believe about God in that moment. My fearful feelings ought to drive me to trust God. When I give in to sinful fear, however, I'm doubting that God really is sovereign, all-powerful, all-loving and good. My thoughts are quickly crowded with unhelpful and untrue things.

Philippians 4 teaches me that the remedy for anxiety is prayer: "Do not be anxious about anything, but in everything by prayer and supplication with thanksgiving let your requests be made known to God" (v. 6). Crying out to the Lord redirects my attention to the only One I truly need to fear and reverence. As Romans 8:31 says, "If God is for us, who can be against us?" Instead of giving in to sinful fear, I want to foster a godly fear that cares only about what my heavenly Father thinks of me. I want faith that trusts him and his love for me, even in the most frightening circumstances. I want to be one of what Scripture terms "Sarah's daughters," following in her faith-filled footsteps as a woman who does what is good and does not "fear anything that is frightening" (1 Peter 3:6).

I've confessed my struggles with sinful fear to my friends and husband many times. One friend encouraged me with this verse from Psalm 34: "I sought the LORD, and he answered me and delivered me from all my fears" (v. 4). Just as the Lord answered David, the Lord will answer us and deliver us from the power of fear. Not only that, but Psalm 34 goes on and invites us to "taste and see" that he is good, to take refuge in him, and to "fear the LORD…for those who fear him have no lack!" (vv. 8-9). God's promises are great to the one who fears him, so why fear anything or anyone else?

AT THE END OF THE DAY

There are some days when I tuck my children into bed knowing I was anything but a stellar mom. If the efficacy of the Gospel were based upon my performance as a mother, I'd flunk that test. Maybe I'm aware of my inconsistency with discipline, or maybe I snapped at someone. Perhaps I'm just ready to run from this parenting thing and escape with a nice soak in the bathtub. Or, it might be all of the above. It's on these days that I'm even more aware of my need for the Gospel than on the days when I feel like I've done a pretty good job.

As I prepare to go to sleep for the night, I'm thankful for the Gospel. I'm thankful that Jesus died on the cross to forgive my sins of a judgmental spirit, my selfishness and my persistent fear. He provided a remedy for my anger and impatience toward my children and for my complaining and self-pitying attitudes. Because Jesus my Savior sits on a throne of grace, I fall asleep forgiven.

Although I feel weak, the Bible tells me that God's power is "made perfect" in my weakness (1 Cor. 12:9). What is my hope and comfort? God is faithful, his steadfast love never ceases, and his "mercies never come to an end; they are new every morning" (Lam. 3:22-23). God's grace is sufficient for today, and he will give me the strength that I need to do all he calls me to do as a mom.

Just let me abide in him. I love these lyrics from Joseph Hart's hymn, *Come, Ye Sinners, Poor and Needy*:

> Come ye sinners, poor and needy,
> Weak and wounded, sick and sore!

> Jesus ready stands to save you,
> Full of pity, love and power...[4]

Whether we realize it or not, we truly are sinners, "poor and needy, weak and wounded, sick and sore." And we really do have a loving Savior "full of pity, love and power."

The same Gospel that first drew us to Jesus invites us to find our refuge, comfort, hope, identity and forgiveness in him on a daily basis. First John 1:8 says, "If we say we have no sin, we deceive ourselves, and the truth is not in us." Let's confess our sins to the one who, as Scripture teaches, is "faithful and just to forgive us our sins and to cleanse us from all unrighteousness" (1 John 1:9).

CHAPTER SEVEN

Mud Pies and Temper Tantrums

When my husband Scott was about four years old, he teamed up with his neighborhood buddy Matthew to play a mean trick on a neighbor girl. Growing up on a cul-de-sac in the 1970's, the kids pretty much ran freely between one another's yards. This particular afternoon, Scott and Matthew took buckets down to a nearby creek, filled them with muddy sand and deposited the goods in this little girl's wading pool while she was in it. Irate, she threatened: "Matthew! Scotty! I'm telling my Daddy, and he's going to throw you in jail!"

Her father really *was* a judge in town, and as far as Scott knew at that tender age, he really *could* have ended up in jail. Immediately overcome by guilt and fear, he ran home.

I remember as a child coveting a piece of dollhouse furniture in the church nursery. I don't remember how I obtained it, but I can still recall the intense guilt I felt for my theft, especially when I was playing with it at a friend's house later that week. Her father was also our pastor, and I could hear him talking in the other room. My conviction led me to confess to him and return the toy.

My mom could tell you about the temper tantrum I threw because she had promised to take me to the library, and when we got there it was closed. Then there was the night I misbehaved with a babysitter and sweetly lied to my parents about my behavior so I could get the treat they had brought home for me.

These are only a few examples from our childhoods. Scott was overcome with conviction of sin when he dumped mud in his neighbor's pool, and I knew I hadn't just borrowed, but actually stolen that piece of dollhouse furniture. Even as a child, I gave in to the sins of anger and lying. You probably have stories of your own. Isn't it amazing that some of our earliest memories point to the sinfulness of our own hearts?

The little ones growing up in our homes are also sinners. Yes, we're the "big sinners," mentioned earlier, but they're still "little sinners." If you're tempted to think that they're just behaving like two-year-olds (or three-year-olds, or four-year-olds, etc.), and thus overlook their sinful behavior, then it's critical that you consider God's Word and what he says about children and their sin. At the same time, let's keep a humble perspective—we too were once "little sinners," and instead of talking down to them, let's remember how we once were young, and how so often we're tempted by—and commit—the same sins today. We just do it in different ways and to different degrees, not to mention being much better at not getting caught.

This is not a book primarily about child training and discipline. There are many good books out there that address that topic, and I have to confess, even though I've read several, I'm still regularly praying for grace to put what I've learned into consistent practice. Nevertheless, loving our children begs a discussion of discipline. So, while I don't intend to expound on the *practice* of child training and discipline, I do want to address the *principle* of child training and discipline by asking some questions. First, why do we discipline? Next, what is our attitude toward discipline? Are we heeding the biblical warnings about it? And finally, how do we approach discipline?

WHY DISCIPLINE?

The simplest answer to this question is that we discipline our children because it is biblical to do so. The Bible talks about discipline as a normal part of the parent-child relationship: "For what son is there whom his father does not discipline? If you are left without discipline, in which all have participated, then you are illegitimate children and not sons" (Heb. 12:7-8). In this context, the author shows how discipline is a model for how God brings us to maturity as Christians. However, he assumes that a loving parent will train and discipline his child in the way he or she should go (Prov. 22:6). Discipline is an important way that we show love to our children.

One of the concrete ways discipline expresses love toward our children is by setting boundaries for their lives. How many of us feel guilty when we say no to our child's requests? Now, I probably say no too often—I'd like to say yes a lot more than I do. Nevertheless, as parents, we have a role in setting boundaries for our children, and part of that job is wisely discerning behaviors and saying both yes and no to a child. This is an act of love.

Take the example that my husband encountered in public. He was waiting in a checkout line with our son John Luke. The cashier started telling him how her brother's two-year-old son was waking up every night around 2:00 a.m. with the same request: "Daddy, I want a hot dog from 7-Eleven." She said that her brother would actually take the boy out, in the middle of the night, and buy him the hot dog!

Maybe we don't buy our children hot dogs in the middle of the night, but isn't it true that sometimes it's just easier to give them what they want than to set boundaries that we know are good for them? What patterns are we establishing by giving into the wishes and whims of our children, especially when many of those wishes have sin at the root?

Maybe you have had bad personal experiences with discipline or have seen it performed in an unloving way. The ultimate purpose of discipline isn't to exert parental domination but to help our children see their need for a Savior. As Paul points out, it's the law that helps us recognize and understand our sinful state: "Yet if it had not been for the law, I would not have known sin. I would not have known what it is to covet if the law had not said, 'You shall not covet'" (Rom. 7:7). We serve our children by establishing boundaries for them, and sometimes that means clearly "laying down the law."

These boundaries should be set by Scripture and not by our own whims or even past experiences. While the Bible is full of instruction on how we ought to live, I find the Ten Commandments particularly helpful. When one of my children lies or steals, it's a black-and-white opportunity to instruct him or her in God's holy law and help that child understand that sowing sinfully will reap unpleasant consequences. It also makes it clear against whom (God) the child is sinning.

As parents of young children, our priority in discipline is to establish authority with them. Both the Old and New Testaments instruct children to obey their parents. We want them to know the good fruit of obedience—not merely for our own convenience, but so that they will experience the promise that life will "go well with them" (Eph. 6:1-3). If they learn obedience at a young age, it will make such a difference in their lives as they relate to other people, especially future employers and other authorities. Even more importantly, though, earthly obedience instructs them in the fear of the Lord who has final authority over the destiny of their eternal souls.

This leads us to the most important "why discipline?" answer in this chapter. When we set boundaries for our children, it soon becomes obvious that the standards underpinning them can't be kept without God's help. None of us can keep the law all the way. "For all have sinned and fall short of the glory of God" (Rom. 3:23). I certainly break God's law every day, and that's why I need a Savior and why my children need a Savior as well.

Helping our children understand their sinful state apart from Christ is a marvelous, albeit challenging, privilege. Until they see their sin, they won't see their need for a Savior. When they acknowledge their guilt, then I can point them to the truth that "God shows his love for us in that while we were still sinners, Christ died for us" (Rom. 5:8). If we love our children, we'll help them recognize sin in their lives and take them to Jesus, the only one who can rescue them from it.

OUR ATTITUDE TOWARD DISCIPLINE

I just described discipline as a *marvelous privilege*. Did you catch that? How does your heart respond to that statement? Do you view discipline as a privilege and opportunity, or is it a dreaded interruption in your day? Too often, I see it as an interruption to my agenda and forget that it is one of the most important parts of my calling as a mom. In fact, it's one of the best ways that I can love my children.

I remember one particular Sunday morning when my husband was serving up front at church. John Luke was a newborn and Elijah was two years old when I attempted to take both boys into the worship service on my own for the singing. There I was, in the back of the high school auditorium where our church met, with infant John Luke strapped to me in a front carrier while I held Elijah's hand firmly.

Eventually, I let go of Elijah's hand and gave him a little more freedom. Well, wouldn't you know, he decided to take a few steps away from me. He turned his little head, smiled with his eyes when I said, "Come," and turned the opposite direction. He then started a run-crawl between legs and seats that I could only hope to follow with John Luke strapped in front of me. Thank goodness for Karen, a friend who caught Elijah in a football hold and held him until I got there. I then proceeded (with baby still in front) to carry a screaming two-year-old out of worship.

Talk about being humbled. Talk about feeling weak. I think that morning cured me from fearing the opinions of others in a church setting. I couldn't imagine my child doing anything worse to get attention in a public meeting. In that moment, I wasn't seeing discipline as a privilege or opportunity, and yet that's exactly what it was. Although Karen could help me catch my son, I was the only one who could address his heart in the following moments.

God ordained that opportunity for my sanctification as well as my son's training. He was more important to me, and his obedience was more important before the Lord, than what anybody in that auditorium might have thought about me leaving worship or his screams in protest. And knowing our church, those who happened to notice (probably not nearly as many as I felt at the time) were probably praying for me and not thinking judgmental thoughts about my parenting at all. Most of them were probably recalling similar parenting moments!

Whether we're at home or in public, let's not be surprised by sin in children or embarrassed by their behavior. Is their sin convenient? Almost never. We might need to leave a grocery cart full of groceries to take a defiant child home. That's okay. That moment is a unique privilege given to us as parents, and, really, it's a very short season before our children will be adults and turned over to the Lord's discipline. In the meantime, we must do all we can to prepare them for that day.

BIBLICAL WARNINGS

Another important part of discipline has to do with being aware of its pitfalls. Are we heeding the biblical warnings surrounding this responsibility? Three such warnings come to mind. First, "Fathers, do not provoke your children to anger, but bring them up in the discipline and instruction of the Lord" (Eph. 6:3). Paul indicates that this is especially likely to function between a father and son, but it has a broader application. So, are we guilty of provoking our children to anger?

When we (or our husbands) use rude, sarcastic, or belittling language, we provoke them. When we do all of the talking and none of the listening, we provoke them. And when we discipline based on our own whims, preferences and comforts rather than God's Word, our hypocritical training often provokes our older children to anger when they grow up and see it for what it is.

Or, are you still struggling with the very concept of discipline, of doing anything at all when faced with a child's sin? It's much easier (in the short term) to abdicate responsibility, but heed the following warning to the parent who neglects discipline this way. "The rod and reproof give wisdom, but a child left to himself brings shame to his mother" (Prov. 29:15).

There is a sowing and reaping principle identified throughout Scripture: You reap what you sow. If you sow good seed, you reap good fruit. If you sow bad seed, you reap bad fruit. The same is true in parenting: If you faithfully pursue your child with the rod of discipline and wise, timely reproof, you reap wisdom for your child. But if you neglect your child's discipline, you reap shame, certainly for you, and likely for your child as well.

Please note that the sowing and reaping principle is not a simplistic formula. It *doesn't* mean we can demand guarantees of outcomes from God based on our actions. There are many choices and circumstances that interact and bear fruit in a person's life. This principle *does* mean that we're called to be faithful with the wise principles God has revealed. Then, we can rest in leaving the ultimate outcome to him.

Finally, Jesus addresses head-on the parent who doesn't simply neglect discipline, but actually leads a child into sinful behavior. "'...whoever causes one of these little ones who believe in me to sin, it would be better for him to have a great millstone fastened around his neck and to be drowned in the depth of the sea'" (Matt. 18:6). This is serious. Jesus isn't holding anything back.

While the term "little ones" in this verse primarily refers to Jesus' followers who exhibit childlike faith in him, how much more do his words apply to how we deal with the spiritual lives of children in our care! If we knowingly and intentionally lead our children into sinful behavior, we'll face serious eternal consequences from the Lord.

AN APPROACH TO DISCIPLINE

So, how do we approach discipline? A few pages ago, I said that I wasn't going to address the *practice* of discipline, so what do I mean by an *approach* to discipline? How we approach something involves more than just coming up with a strategy; it speaks to the general frame of mind we find ourselves in when parenting. As such, there's one little nugget of wisdom that I just don't want to miss sharing with you.

When Scott and I were in the hospital with our firstborn, I remember feeling overwhelmed by the task of parenting that was ahead of me. We asked our senior pastor for his thoughts, and he said that the one piece of counsel he would give us was that, just like everything else in the Christian life, parenting children is best done by faith. That's a sound approach.

There have been countless times when the Lord has encouraged and strengthened our souls by reminding us of this simple and profound truth. Parent by faith. From those early parenting, middle-of-the-night cries and prayers for wisdom beside our bed to the cries and prayers that we send up when one of our kids is struggling with something today, we feel our weakness and realize our dependence on the Lord to parent our children.

It's in these times that the Lord reminds us that no method will work all the time, and no method will ultimately save souls. We are thankful for them, but methods do not have inherent power to change lives as only God can. Christian parenting is by faith because the Christian life is one lived by faith in Christ. By faith, we ask God to help us. He graciously promises to give wisdom generously to those who ask him (James 1:5).

EVEN MOSQUITOES

Scott had to leave the house early one morning to meet a friend for breakfast, so it was my responsibility to lead our family devotional time. As the kids munched on bananas and Cheerios, I read this from our storybook Bible:

> God wrote, "I love you"—he wrote it in the sky, and on the earth, and under the sea. He wrote his message everywhere! Because God created everything in his world to reflect him like a mirror—to show us what he is like, to help us know him, to make our hearts sing. The way a kitten chases her tail. The way red poppies grow wild. The way a dolphin swims.[5]

In that moment, even though I was reading to my children, the Lord and I were having a heart-to-heart conversation. As I read the truth that God made everything in creation to point to himself in some way, do you know what my first question was? "What about mosquitoes, God? How do they reflect your glory?" I wasn't expecting a response. But immediately, in my mind, I pictured the way mosquitoes swarm around my son Elijah.

For some reason, our backyard at the time was a mosquito breeding ground, and my son is one of those boys with sweet meat whom the mosquitoes just can't get enough of. When he's bitten, the poor guy gets quarter-sized welts on his arms and legs. (And he gets plenty of them!)

This might be a stretch for those of you who, like me, would be happy if there were no such thing as a mosquito. Stay with me. That morning, I thought the Lord was giving me a picture to help me see how even mosquitoes reflect his glory. No matter what you do to try to get rid of the pests, they keep coming at you. They're persistent, never giving up. You think they're gone, and then you hear one buzzing in your ear.

Yes, even a mosquito portrays an aspect of God's character—because God is just like that. No matter how hard we try to resist his discipline, keep him away or get rid of him, he persistently and patiently pursues us. We're his children, and he pursued us all the way to the cross. It's at Calvary where he showcases his love and mercy toward us.

As we discipline and train our children, we might sometimes feel like mosquitoes. Maybe our kids think we're like mosquitoes--annoying and bothersome, interrupting their plans and agendas, redirecting them and pointing out truths they'd rather ignore. At those times, let's reflect on our heavenly Father who patiently, faithfully and lovingly pursues us to the end. Let's never give up on our kids, and let's love them with discipline that helps them see their need for a Savior and points them to the Gospel.

CHAPTER EIGHT

What We See and What We Say

This book is about loving our children. So far, we've looked at the idea that the best way to love them is with the Gospel, and one of the best gifts we can give them is to love their father. We considered God's particular design in making our children the way he did, and we marveled at his sovereignty in choosing us to be their parents and them to be our children. We also looked at the importance of addressing sin in our own hearts and in the hearts of our children. Now, let's get even more personal. We're going to discuss our eyes and our tongues—what we see when we look at our children and what we say to them and about them when we speak.

Have you ever heard of the Coxsackie virus? It's also

known as Hand, Foot and Mouth Disease (HFM). It often brings a fever, loss of appetite and exhaustion. One summer, two of my boys caught it. I thought the worst part was when they got blisters in their mouths. The painful sores made it hard to swallow the liquids they needed so badly. When the virus was on its way out, it left a rash that blistered their hands and feet. Even a month later, my husband and I saw the effects of the virus as their fingernails and toenails started peeling.

When I think about the role our eyes and tongues play in parenting, a virus comes to mind. If we aren't careful, it's easy for us to put down our guard and use our eyes and our tongues, designed for godly purposes, in harmful and hurtful ways. Our vision can become increasingly near-sighted, and our tongues can become poisonous to ourselves and others. It's very much like a disease process.

So, I want to pose some questions. First, let's talk about our eyes. What do we see when we look at our children? What lenses are we using? Are we more aware of their weaknesses or of God's grace at work in their lives? Is our vision for them near-sighted or far-sighted?

Next, the tongue demands our attention. How do we talk to our children? What do we say about our children to others? Are we prone to gossip or boasting? How do we approach seeking others for counsel about our children?

WHAT WE SEE

Let's start by exploring the role of our eyes. When I started writing this book, I took a good look at my then two-year-old, John Luke. I saw a bundle of energy. I saw his tousled hair, huge grin, and bright blue eyes that were full of laughter. I also noticed the piece of cereal glued with milk to his backside. "All boy," as they say, he was eager to help his daddy fix the car. He would swing with his Wiffle ball bat at pitches all morning. He wouldn't even notice when his head bumped the dining room table if he took a running curve a little too fast.

While I saw a lot of the little boy emerging, he was still pretty attached to me. He snuggled next to me with his apple juice in the morning, and if he saw me typing on my laptop computer, he pushed it away and scooted onto my lap, right between me and the screen. There's a lot to love about this boy! At the same time, he was definitely a two-year-old, and Scott and I were increasingly aware of some of his particular weaknesses and temptations. It's not easy being the little brother, and we knew that soon he would be faced with another set of challenges with the arrival of a new sibling. I needed the Lord to give me insight to help me see this little guy the way he sees him.

WHAT KIND OF GLASSES ARE WE WEARING?

When we think about how we see our children, there are

three different lenses through which we might be viewing them: rose-colored glasses, sharp-nosed spectacles or X-ray lenses. First, rose-colored glasses are tinted, and when we look through them we see our children the way we (or perhaps even others) want to see them. Sharp-nosed spectacles are glasses belonging to a parent who looks at her children with a fault-finding, critical eye. Finally, X-ray lenses are glasses that allow a mom to look past the outward appearance into the heart of her child.

Imagine, on one end of the spectrum, a mother wearing rose-colored glasses. This mom is blind to the truth (especially the uglier aspects of it) and never sees anything wrong in her son, never corrects him and thinks only the best of everything he does. She doesn't question his friendships or consider where seemingly innocent liberties and youthful passions might lead him in adulthood.

Fast forward several years, and when that son grows up, he doesn't even see that he's proud and arrogant and rudely walks over anyone in his path. He can't handle criticism of any kind. And authority figures? They get only lip service (to avoid trouble) and rarely see the seething, boiling lakes of discontent beneath the surface until it's too late.

By comparison, imagine a mother wearing sharp-nosed spectacles. She's at the other end of the spectrum. Naturally inclined to be judgmental, her critical eye is always finding fault with her two daughters about everything from their behavior, to their appearances, to their schoolwork. She's controlling, establishing strict rules in the home that give her daughters no freedom and cripple them emotionally rather than helping them prepare for biblical independence.

No wonder she's shocked and humiliated when the younger daughter rebels, leaving home to live with her boyfriend. By comparison, the older daughter never leaves home, mortally afraid of crossing the will of her mother, craving her approval.

Both the mom wearing rose-colored glasses and the mom wearing sharp-nosed spectacles have something important in common. They're looking at outward appearances. One mother finds no fault, and the other finds *only* fault. The examples I invented are extreme, but perhaps you can find yourself closer to one end of the spectrum than the other. I hope they illustrate what we don't want to be like so that we're better prepared to look at our children through X-ray lenses, a supernatural feat that only God can help us do.

When the prophet Samuel went to anoint one of Jesse's sons to be the next king of Israel, the Lord made it clear that he doesn't see people the way man observes and judges them. "For the LORD sees not as man sees: man looks on the outward appearance, but the LORD looks on the heart" (1 Sam. 16:7). It takes the discernment of the Holy Spirit to look at our children's hearts with understanding.

WEAKNESS OR GRACE

On a daily basis, I need to check my own heart and ask the Lord to help me see my children with his eyes. In 1 Peter 3:7, Peter instructs husbands to live with their wives "in an understanding way." I can't tell you how many times this phrase has come to mind as I consider my children. Although this command is primarily intended for husbands, I think it could only do us good to live with our children in an understanding way as well. It's wise for us to study them—to learn what makes them happy and excited, to know their preferences, and to be aware of their particular strengths as well as sinful tendencies.

A temptation for me with my children is to see more of their weaknesses and sin struggles than I do of God's grace at work in their lives. Now, as moms, we have a unique perspective and God-ordained insight into the characters of our children that, wisely applied, is meant to bring them good and not harm. But in being vigilant and speaking into their lives, it is prudent to be more aware of God's grace than of their weaknesses.

When I give my son an instruction and he obeys but doesn't say "yes, Mommy" like I've taught him to respond, am I more grateful that he's learning to obey in general, or disgruntled because he forgot to say a particular phrase?

109

Or, when my toddler squeezes my legs, do I welcome this enthusiastic affection or do I immediately ask him to be gentle with me? At the end of the day, are we more aware of a daughter's conscious choice to obey and be helpful at the grocery store in the morning or her need for discipline when she gets home, tired and hungry?

Overall, am I thanking God for growth, even as I see areas where my children still need to grow? We can have such short memories for grace at work and clogged memory banks full of shortcomings. There's a call for patience in motherhood. Our children don't stop wearing diapers and go right off to college. There's a physical and social maturing process that takes place over time. In the same way, change doesn't happen overnight in anyone. We need discernment to recognize when our children are just being children and when there's a sinful pattern that we are positioned to address and correct. This calls for dependent prayer that trusts God to work change in his time and rejoices in his grace along the way.

NEAR-SIGHTED OR FAR-SIGHTED

Are we near-sighted or far-sighted when we look at our children? In his essay titled *The Weight of Glory,* Christian thinker and writer C.S. Lewis describes how one day, when our Lord returns, we will see one another for who we really are. All the trappings of earth and sinful flesh will be stripped away, and our true souls and renewed bodies will be revealed. In the meantime, we all walk around with limited vision, only seeing one another dimly, largely undervaluing the work that God is doing in sanctifying lives.[6]

As I look at my children, I want to see past their dirty fingernails, sweaty hair and stinky feet. I want to see past their weakness and sin. These little bodies carry eternal souls, and I want to see not only who my children are right now, but also who they will one day be. And not just twenty or even fifty years from now on earth, but who they will be in eternity. My hope and prayer is that they will love Jesus and be with him in heaven, glorified and free from all sins forever. What a privilege it is to love and nurture and encourage and strengthen eternal souls! Let's ask the Lord to give us his vision as we look at our children.

WHAT WE SAY

If how we see matters, then how much more do the words that we speak matter? This concept of seeing correctly leads right into what we say to and about our children, because what I see goes into my heart, and what's in my heart comes out of my mouth (Matt. 12:34). If I see my children as small, eternal souls entrusted to my care, then I will guard my mouth as I deal with them.

James, the brother of Jesus, has a lot to say about our tongues. He identifies the tongue as "a fire," a "world of unrighteousness," "a restless evil," "full of deadly poison" and utterly untamable. He invites us to consider that "From the same mouth come blessing and cursing. ... These things ought not to be so" (James 3:10).

Picture a mom in the middle of an angry conflict with her children when the telephone rings. How long does it take her to compose herself and sweetly answer, "Hello, how are you..." to the person on the other end of the line? Or, consider the husband and wife who have an argument on the way to church on a Sunday morning and aren't speaking to one another, and then put on smiles as they greet their friends in the church lobby. Why is it that we can practice self-control in our conversations with those outside of our families, but then find it so hard to be self-controlled with our tongues in our own homes?

James sheds some light on the matter when he says that "no human being can tame the tongue" (James 3:8). Although it's a small part of the body, like a tiny match, it can set ablaze a great forest. So maybe you're thinking, "So *that's* why it's so hard to keep my mouth shut. If no human being can tame the tongue, then I'm off the hook, right? It's beyond my control."

Not quite. By raising the issue, James is implying that there is a necessary solution. There is a way that sinful tongues can in fact be tamed—by the power of the Holy Spirit. It's a miracle of God's gracious work in a believer's life. Galatians lists self-control among the fruits of the Spirit that those who belong to Christ display. So, while we can't tame the tongue by ourselves, we are called to crucify the flesh with its passions and desires, including the tongue and its works.

In light of all that Christ has accomplished on our behalf through the cross, we're to present our bodies as living sacrifices, "holy and acceptable to God" (Rom. 12:1). It's through this act of humble submission that the Holy Spirit sanctifies us, transforming even our tongues. It's the Spirit who teaches us to speak self-controlled, pure, true, pleasing and God-glorifying words.

TALKING TO OUR CHILDREN

Moms, we're ladies, so let's face it: most of us like to talk. Some of us like to talk a lot. Because of this tendency, we need to address the tone and content of our words.

First, how do we speak to our children? What kind of tone do we use with them? Are we loud or quiet? Do we speak down to them, using vocabulary or jargon that they might not yet understand, or do we speak at their level, adapting our language to what they can comprehend? Do we talk too much or do we take time to listen to what they say?

This is a good time to ask our husbands or maybe some close friends to tell us what they observe in our speech. Depending on the ages of our children, it might be good to ask *them* what they hear when we speak. We might be surprised by another's perspective on this.

Have you ever heard your voice recorded and thought, "That can't be me. That's not what I sound like at all!" Just as it's not uncommon for us to hear ourselves differently with our physical ears, it shouldn't surprise us if our children think we sound harsh, even if we think our communication is fine.

So what about the content of our conversations with our children? Words are powerful. God spoke, and everything came to be. Created in God's image, our words are also powerful in human relationships.[7] How are we using them? Are we speaking words that build up or tear down?

Proverbs 14:1 says, "The wisest of women builds her house, but folly with her own hands tears it down." As moms, we want to "build up" the children living in our homes and not tear them down, but what do our words communicate to them? Are we regularly encouraging and speaking truth to them? Or, are we the ones who are attacking and discouraging them?

When my husband and I were engaged, we asked Scott's parents what counsel they could give us. They encouraged us to make our relationship—and ultimately our home—a safe place for one another. What a simple, amazing gift! We want to extend this same protection to our children. A fallen world is not likely to be friendly to them, but our home can be a wonderful refuge where they find understanding and grace, where truth is spoken and encouragement reigns.

TALKING ABOUT OUR CHILDREN

Next, what do we say to others about our children and how do we say it? If one of our children were in the room, would we speak differently? If he or she is in the room, are we mindful of what our words might communicate, what impact they might have? We know gossip is sin, but does it apply to talking about our children? The answer is *yes*. Loving our children includes both protecting and respecting them. Even a funny story about what a child said or did might embarrass him or her when shared publicly. It's wise to consider the audience, and, in certain cases, it may be wise to ask the child first if sharing a story about him or her is okay.

With that in mind, there's a place for seeking godly counsel from others that doesn't fall under the heading of gossip. If we do so in agreement with our spouses, it's healthy to go to a trusted friend, a godly couple or an accountability group and ask for help in parenting, as long as we keep the main purpose in mind and our hearts are in a good place as regards that child. Ultimately, a mother should have her child's best interest at heart. We also need to go humbly, meaning that we shouldn't just make quick assumptions about a child's guilt or motivations. We should have a healthy level of doubt as to our own interpretation of facts.

We're ultimately after the truth, so we need to be open to seeing our own contribution to a conflict with our child or how we're currently addressing our child's weakness or sin. And sometimes, we simply get the facts wrong, and we need to acknowledge when we do.

Another sin that moms are tempted to commit in conversations about their children is boasting. And this can be quite subtle…or not! (There's a reason grandmothers have so-called "brag books" in their purses, with photos ready to whip out at a moment's notice!) Instead of boasting about wisdom, abilities or wealth, Jeremiah teaches us to boast in the Lord: "…let him who boasts boast in this, that he understands and knows me, that I am the LORD" (Jer. 9:24).

Each child is a good gift from the Lord, and it is right to give thanks to God for the unique talents and abilities with which he blesses our children. We also want to be cheerleaders for them, encouraging them when they develop and use their gifts in ways that please and honor the Lord. But does our speech point to the Lord and acknowledge his grace at work in their lives, or do we, as moms, give in to a kind of sinful boasting that focuses too much on our children and their accomplishments (and maybe even our role in their accomplishments)? Who's being glorified here?

Something else to watch for is how much of the talking we're doing in any given conversation. Are we just as interested in asking about other children as we are in talking about our own? Quantity of words, when talking with others, can be a good indicator of where our hearts are, or where they're about to head.

WISDOM AND KINDNESS

Here's an excellent proverb to keep in mind. In Proverbs 31, the extolled woman "opens her mouth with wisdom, and the teaching of kindness is on her tongue" (v. 26). Even more, if we are redeemed daughters of our Lord, may we put on wise speech and kindness as we talk to and about our children. Remember, the best way we can love our children is by passing on the Gospel to them. We want to do this not only with our words, but also by the example of our lives. Paul urges the Colossians to "put to death" and "put away" sin. Instead, Christians are to "put on…as God's chosen ones, holy and beloved, compassion, kindness, humility, meekness, and patience" (Col. 3:12).

As those saved by grace, let's put on compassionate, kind, humble, meek and patient words as we interact with our children. Let's listen to their questions, point them to the Savior, and not distract or detract from what he's doing in their hearts. Keeping in mind that these active little bodies running around our homes hold eternal souls, let's use our words carefully to prepare them for the future, giving them a vision for eternity with Jesus and others in heaven.

HE IS ABLE

One of the things I hope you've heard as you've read this chapter is that apart from God's grace, we are all prone to temptation when it comes to loving our children with our eyes and our mouths. We're all at different places in learning to put to death our sin nature and allowing the Lord to give us eyes to really see our children the way he does and to talk to them in ways that edify them and bring glory to Christ.

Perhaps you're feeling stuck. You want to see past your child's weaknesses to God's grace at work, and you just can't. You want to put to death old patterns of speech, but they don't die easily. It seems as if for every hundred times a day you hold back that angry word, there seem to be ten that escape your lips, and sadly, those ten are the ones that play back in your head as you're trying to fall asleep at night.

May Paul's prayer for the Ephesians encourage you: "Now to him who is able to do far more abundantly than all that we ask or think, according to the power at work within us, to him be glory in the church and in Christ Jesus through-out all generations, forever and ever. Amen" (Eph. 3:20-21). God is not finished with you—or your children—yet. He is "able to do far more abundantly than all that we ask or think" both in our lives and in their lives. If we're in Christ, we can rest in the promise that God will complete the good work that he began in us when he first called us to himself (Phil. 1:6).

Our confidence is based not on what we're able to do for ourselves or for our children, but it's based on what Christ is able to do, and, more importantly, what he's already ac-complished on the cross. His power is at work within us, for his glory, forever.

CHAPTER NINE

This Momentary Motherhood

Anticipation turns into action when a baby is on the way. Schedules fill with medical appointments, childbirth or parenting classes, adoption paperwork, a baby shower or even a move to a new home. For our family, a new baby means rearranging bedrooms. We set up the cradle that my father first built for Elijah, and I think of his loving hands sanding it as I wash off the dust. I put away newborn diapers, buy hypoallergenic laundry detergent, and bring little baby clothes out of storage. I picture little fingers and a tiny body that will soon fill the one-piece outfits as I fold the clean laundry.

Before Elijah was born, I took several walks with my friend Melanie. Because he was our first, I picked her brain about everything I could think of regarding child care and training. In addition to taking a labor and delivery class at the hospital, Scott and I attended a parenting seminar that our church hosted. We read lots of books about pregnancy, childcare and child training.

The day Elijah actually entered the world, all of my plans for a natural delivery and smooth adjustment to breastfeeding went out the window. When my doctor told me I needed to have an emergency C-section, I realized that somehow I'd neglected to read that chapter in any of my books! Then it took Scott and me several weeks of watching Elijah struggle to put on weight before we realized why breastfeeding was so challenging. As it turned out, Elijah was severely tongue-tied, and he needed a surgical procedure to fix the issue. Even though neither labor and delivery nor feeding went the way Scott and I had planned, we experienced God's amazing faithfulness and kindness, and we learned to press into him in prayer.

Prior to John Luke's birth, one of my greatest concerns had to do with the transition from one to two children. With a stay-at-home mom, Elijah was accustomed to having my undivided attention so much of the time. How would he handle sharing me with another person? How could I, as a mom, love my second child as much as the first? My mom told me that when you have one child, it's hard to imagine ever being able to share your love with another little one. Then, when that second child comes, your love multiplies.

She told me that you don't love either child less, but you love both more.

Now, with Silas and Selah added, Scott and I are definitely outnumbered! When I'm home alone with my children, I only have two hands to serve four little ones. But my mom's words have proven true, and, over time, not only do I love each of my children more, but I've come to see what a good gift each child is to our whole family.

Just as winter turns to spring, and summer to fall, the seasons of our lives change. Whether you are welcoming your first or your seventh baby, real change occurs when a new little life enters the home. Sometimes things go the way you plan, sometimes they don't. In each season, though, God's grace is sufficient and his mercies are new. While loving my children can be hard work and doesn't always come naturally, I'm learning to slow down and savor the sweetness of my current season of life. As our children grow and mature, there are more seasons to come.

LONG DAYS, SHORT YEARS

Has anyone ever told you, "The days are long, but the years are short"? I've heard these words repeated many times, and I believe them. As mothers of young children, our days can feel very long, and it can be hard to see an end to wiping runny noses and messy bottoms. Yet, for most of us, while we're moms for life, this season of parenting small children is relatively short, only a fraction of our lives. And these same years represent some of the most formative and significant years in a child's development. So for a few minutes, let's lift our eyes from the playroom floor and ponder what this means.

As I mentioned to earlier, Scripture talks about seasons of life. It also teaches a sowing and reaping principle. A farmer sows his seed in one season, the crops grow and mature in another and finally they bear fruit at harvest time. The seasons of sowing and reaping in our lives function the same way. If we sow bad seed, we will one day reap bad fruit. If we sow good seed, we will one day reap good fruit.

Paul's encouragement to the Galatians seems especially applicable to mothers with young children. He says, "And let us not grow weary of doing good, for in due season we will reap, if we do not give up" (Gal. 6:9). As mothers of young children, we are in a season of sowing, and we most likely will not see immediate fruit of either character or spiritual vitality. Part of loving our children is staying the course, not giving up. We're in this for the long haul!

Though sweet, the season of nurturing young children can be a particularly tiring one. It's often physically taxing because we're doing everything for our little ones—putting them in car seats, changing their diapers (or supervising the potty), dressing them, shopping for them, cooking for them and cleaning up their messes. We're at least slightly sleep-deprived all the time.

I once heard Christian writer and pastor C.J. Mahaney make an important distinction: being tired is not the same as being weary. Tiredness is normal and comes with busy seasons of life. Weariness, however, is a matter of the heart. When Paul talks to the Galatians, he's telling them not to "grow *weary* of doing good" (emphasis mine). All these things that we're doing for our children are included in this category of "doing good." We are sacrificially serving our families. But how are we serving them? Are we serving with bodies that are simply tired, or are some of our hearts growing weary?

If you are feeling weary, please find encouragement in the second half of the verse: "...for in due season we will reap, if we do not give up." The little ones that we care for day in and day out might not even be able to say the words "thank you," but the Bible promises that there is eternal reward for these everyday, mundane acts of service.

Maybe the weariness sets in when I'm wiping that same runny nose for the tenth time in one hour. The Lord reminds me that, if I wipe that nose for his glory, that seemingly meaningless act has eternal value: "Whatever you do, work heartily, as for the Lord and not for men, knowing that from the Lord you will receive the inheritance as your reward. You are serving the Lord Christ" (1 Cor. 3:23-24).

How do I fight weariness? I fight weariness by meditating on the truth that I'm not only serving my children, but the Lord. He gives purpose to an act of service to a little one.

Let's get more practical. It can be hard to lift the eyes of our hearts to meditate on biblical truth when our physical eyes are glued to a toddler running around the playground. Sometimes we need other people around us to remind us of vital truths. The first person on our list should be our husbands. Or, if not married, godly friends or spiritual leaders. Then, in accordance with Titus 2, it's invaluable to have a more seasoned woman in our lives to encourage and counsel us on a regular basis. It's also helpful to have a friend or other couple walking through the same season so that we can mutually encourage and spur one another on to parent for God's glory. These are hard roads that God never intended us to walk alone. We benefit when we embrace the gift of Christian community.

FUTURE BLESSING

Although our toddlers probably won't literally rise up and bless us verbally, perhaps one day we'll be like the Proverbs 31 woman who sowed well and reaped the fruit of praise: "Her children rise up and call her blessed; ... give her the fruit of her hands, and let her works praise her in the gates" (vv. 28, 31). Even if others don't see our labors, our Father in heaven sees the good we are doing, and he will reward us. We live for his "Well done, good and faithful servant."

While God has blessed me richly in friendships with many godly women who now have grown children, my mom stands out among the rest. The reason my mom's life is full of good things is because she did not grow weary of doing good. She stayed the course. A true Titus 2 woman, she has devoted herself to loving her husband and children. She logged 18 years with at least one infant or preschooler in tow, and she spent 20 years as a homeschool mom. I can only guess how many diapers she's changed (the cloth kind, mind you), meals she's cooked, Bible verses she's taught and nights she's stayed awake praying for her children. But the Lord "kept count of her tossings" and he put her "tears in [his] bottle" (Ps. 56:8). None of her service or suffering on our behalf went unnoticed. Now, she's beginning to reap some of the fruit of her years of faithful sowing.

At the beginning of this book, I said that the best way to love our children is to pass the Gospel on to them. All five of her children confess Jesus as Lord and Savior. I said that the best gift you can give your children is to love their father. Although not perfectly, my mom and dad have loved one another faithfully, and their marriage is a picture of the Gospel. My mom embraces God's sovereignty over the lives of her children, celebrates the gift of children, and has been an example of confessing her own sin and asking for our forgiveness.

She's trained, disciplined and counseled each one of our sinful hearts. Most of all, the Lord has done a great work in saving her through the Gospel and using motherhood to sanctify her. My mother would be the first to confess her weakness when it comes to parenting, and she'd be the first to point to the Lord's mercy and grace at work in the lives of her children.

My mom worked hard, and she was often tired, but her labors were not in vain. She worked as if God were her only audience, and while she is experiencing some of the good fruit of her hands now, her reward will be in heaven. By God's grace, the same promise is true for us. In due season we will reap, if we do not give up.

In the meantime, as we wait for that future day, I want to capture and enjoy today. I want to hear each ticklish giggle, marvel at the tiny toenails I'm clipping, display lavish affection, listen to the stories, kiss the wounds, wipe the tears, sing, pray and play with my children. The days are long, but the years are short. I want to see, savor and redeem each moment.

THE LOVE CHAPTER

The thirteenth chapter of 1 Corinthians is often called the "Love Chapter." Squeezed right between two chapters addressing the use of spiritual gifts, it eloquently champions the primacy of love in all relationships. A beautiful passage of Scripture, there's good reason it's often read at weddings.

Let's look at it as mothers of young children. "If I speak in the tongues of men and of angels, but have not love, I am a noisy gong or a clanging cymbal" (v. 1). How about this? If I give my children a lot of advice, but have not love, I will just sound like the teacher in a Peanuts cartoon. "Wah wah wah wah wah wah."

Paul continues, "And if I have prophetic powers, and understand all mysteries and all knowledge, and if I have all faith, so as to remove mountains, but have not love, I am nothing. If I give away all I have, and if I deliver up my body to be burned, but have not love, I gain nothing" (vv. 2-3). What if I know the answers to all of my children's questions, attend every sporting event and drive my children to every music lesson? If I don't love them, I am nothing. If I can give each child a college education, or even go so far as to die for one of them, but I act without love, then my sacrifice is meaningless.

Diapers will pass away, and piles of laundry will cease. Parenting books will gather dust on the shelves. We train and parent to the best of our ability, but one day, we'll see the big picture.

Ultimately, love matters most: "Love is patient and kind;

love does not envy or boast; it is not arrogant or rude. It does not insist on its own way; it is not irritable or resentful; it does not rejoice at wrong-doing, but rejoices with the truth. Love bears all things, believes all things, hopes all things, endures all things. ... So now faith, hope, and love abide, these three; but the greatest of these is love" (vv. 4-7, 13). May the Lord give all of us grace to love our children well—for his glory, and for their good.

NOTES

CHAPTER THREE

[1] John Piper, "Manhood, Womanhood, and God, Parts 1-4," audio messages, September 20-22, 1993 (http://www.desiringgod.org/re-source-library/conference-messages).

CHAPTER FOUR

[2] D. Martyn Lloyd-Jones, *Spiritual Depression: Its Causes and Cure* (Grand Rapids: Eerdmans, 1965), 20-21.

CHAPTER FIVE

[3] *The New International Webster's Comprehensive Dictionary of the English Language* (Naples: Trident Press International, 1999), 1201.

CHAPTER SIX

[4] Joseph Hart, "Come, Ye Sinners, Poor and Needy," *The Hymnal for Worship and Celebration* (Waco: Word Music, 1986), 334.

CHAPTER SEVEN

[5] Sally Lloyd-Jones, *The Jesus Storybook Bible* (Grand Rapids: Zondervan, 2007), 12.

CHAPTER EIGHT

[6] C.S. Lewis, *The Weight of Glory: And Other Addresses* (New York: Harper Collins, 2001).

[7] I am indebted to Paul Tripp for this idea. Paul Tripp, *War of Words: Getting to the Heart of Your Communication Struggles*, (Phillipsburg: P & R Publishing, 2000).

CPSIA information can be obtained at www.ICGtesting.com
Printed in the USA
BVOW05s1212120715

408437BV00014B/232/P

9 780615 975528